THE
COMPLETE
BOOK OF
AUSTRALIAN
FINCHES

Distributed in the UNITED STATES to the Pet Trade by T.F.H. Publications, Inc., One T.F.H. Plaza, Neptune City, NJ 07753; distributed in the UNITED STATES to the Bookstore and Library Trade by National Book Network, Inc. 4720 Boston Way, Lanham MD 20706; in CANADA to the Pet Trade by H & L Pet Supplies Inc., 27 Kingston Crescent, Kitchener, Ontario N2B 2T6; Rolf C. Hagen Ltd., 3225 Sartelon Street, Montreal 382 Quebec; in CANADA to the Book Trade by Vanwell Publishing Ltd., 1 Northrup Crescent, St. Catharines, Ontario L2M 6P5 ; in ENGLAND by T.F.H. Publications, PO Box 15, Waterlooville PO7 6BQ; in AUSTRALIA AND THE SOUTH PACIFIC by T.F.H. (Australia), Pty. Ltd., Box 149, Brookvale 2100 N.S.W., Australia; in NEW ZEALAND by Brooklands Aquarium Ltd. 5 McGiven Drive, New Plymouth, RD1 New Zealand; in Japan by T.F.H. Publications, Japan—Jiro Tsuda, 10-12-3 Ohjidai, Sakura, Chiba 285, Japan; in SOUTH AFRICA by Lopis (Pty) Ltd., P.O. Box 39127, Booysens, 2016, Johannesburg, South Africa. Published by T.F.H. Publications, Inc.
MANUFACTURED IN THE UNITED STATES OF AMERICA
BY T.F.H. PUBLICATIONS, INC.

THE COMPLETE BOOK OF AUSTRALIAN FINCHES

A. J. MOBBS

Introduction by Robin Restall

Photographs by Cyril Laubscher
and the Author

Photo credits
The publishers would like to express their thanks to the following for kindly providing pictures:
To Cyril Laubscher for all color photographs with the exception of four provided by the author (listed below); and for black-and-white photographs on pages 8, 9, 12, 21, 29, 39, 40, 43, 44 (both), 46, 47, 48, 53, 56 (both), 57, 61, 65, 67 top right, 69, 70, 74, 77, 79, 81, 84, 89, 92, 93, 96, 110, 116, 125, 136 top, 141, 143, 144.
To the author for color photographs on pages 18 bottom, 30 top left, 30 top right, 127 bottom; and for black-and-white photographs on pages 13, 14, 15 (both), 28, 32, 33 (both), 34, 36–37, 38, 66, 67 top left, 67 bottom, 72, 75 (both), 98, 103, 104 (both), 105, 107, 120 (both), 121, 131, 133 (both), 135, 136 bottom, 138 (both).

Acknowledgement is also given to all those (in addition to the author) who have kindly helped by allowing their birds to be photographed, or who have otherwise assisted in arranging subjects:

Keith Bailey, Eric Barlow, Peter and Joan Barnes, Fred Barnicoat, Trevor Bonneywell, Roy and Debbie Coster, Bill Dobbs, Alan Donnelly, Mike Fidler, Rolf Gudegast, John and Marilyn Horton, Jean Kozicka, Wally Last, Errol Laubscher, Ken and Jean Lawrence, Keith Mannering, Bob Oliver, Les Perry, Oreste Piotto, Mick and Beryl Plose, Harry Porter, Val and Brian Reed, Eric Shipperbottom, Dave Taylor, Sid and Ann Timms, Joyce Venner and Chris Wellings.

CONTENTS

To DAVID and KATE

Editor: Lesley Young
Designer: Carole Perks

INTRODUCTION

The small group of birds known as Australian finches are representatives of three subfamilies of the Estrildidae. The Yellow-rumped Finch and Chestnut-breasted Finch are in the Lonchuri, genus *Lonchura*, while the Pictorella Finch, one of the oldest species of Estrildid in evolutionary terms, is usually accorded its own special subfamily Heteromuni, but I think it is reasonable to include it in *Lonchura*. The beautiful parrot finches of the Erythruri, genus *Chloebia*, are represented by the Blue-faced Parrot Finch and the Gouldian Finch. The latter is so colorful that most people, upon seeing it for the first time, have difficulty in believing it is naturally colored.

The remainder form a complete subfamily, the Poephili, or grassfinches. While being superficially similar small seed-eating birds with cone-shaped bills, all beautifully colored in quite different ways, they are subtly different in quite profound ways.

The Australian finches have all been favorites in aviculture for many years. A hundred years ago, Arthur Butler wrote of them with great familiarity. His book *Foreign Finches in Captivity* (1889) still makes the most fascinating reading, and the lithographs by F.W. Frohawk set a standard that is surpassed only by the photographs by Cyril Laubscher and the author in the present volume.

The Australians keep their finches in wonderfully roomy aviaries, planted with tall clumps of wild millet that provide perfectly natural habitats for their birds. Australian keepers have access to termites, and by means of these they have domesticated the exquisite little Painted Finch to the point where it now breeds with the ease and fecundity of the Zebra Finch, without any further need for live food. They don't have it all their own way: Worms are a major problem, cats are a real pest; and drongo-shrikes, hunting in pairs, can terrorize an aviary of finches and rip bits of them through the wire. Australian finches behave somewhat differently in their wild habitat from the way they behave in captivity, and in Australian captivity they behave somewhat differently from the way they behave in Europe and America. So a book like this one, which draws attention to the avicultural conditions in Europe and America, is not only of great interest, but is totally relevant.

Despite the fact that Australian finches have been readily available on the market for 150 years or more, it is only in the last 30 years or so that serious attempts have been made to domesticate them. This was quite essential if they were not to die out, for the Australian government has forbidden the export of native species since 1960.

At first market forces played a great part, those species in greatest demand fetching the best prices and receiving the most dedicated attention. However, during the mid-1960s in England, a corps of enthusiasts arose who were much more concerned to establish these birds as strong, healthy, self-perpetuating strains. Having bred Diamond Firetails and the Long-tailed and Heck's Grassfinches myself in earlier days, I concentrated on the difficult Masked Grassfinch and Plum-headed Finch. For a while I was President of the Australian Finch Society. I clearly remember Tony Mobbs as a well-known specialist in hummingbirds then. But he switched to Gouldian Finches and became so expert that he wrote a book, *Gouldian Finches, their Care and Breeding*. Tony added the Bicheno or Owl Finch, an exquisite diminutive little grassfinch, to his collection, and subsequently wrote a fine handbook about this bird also.

I left England in 1967 to travel the world and study the finches of each country in which I lived, only occasionally stopping to work on one of the Australian Finches. Tony Mobbs, however, extended his experience and knowledge to the point where he can now stand as a world authority on the care and breeding of these birds in captivity.

It is to the dedicated aviculturist who has specialized in establishing the rarer forms and species like the black-rumped form of the Bicheno Finch in such a manner as Tony has done, that aviculture can be thankful. Today the Gouldian, or Lady Gould Finch, is now a robust species that will breed without the help and assistance of the Society Finch. It can winter in warm, sensible, draftproof quarters without having to be mollycoddled in tropical conditions. The Rufous-tailed Finch or Star Finch is available in a beautiful yellow variant, and a fawn variant of the Chestnut-breasted Finch has appeared. It is a very compact, yet fascinating branch of aviculture that fully rewards those interested in it, and in many ways it is only at the beginning.

ROBIN RESTALL

A

ACCOMMODATION
It is most important to have suitable accommodation ready before purchasing Australian finches. To purchase birds on impulse without first giving a thought as to where you are going to house them can prove disastrous both for you and for the birds.

Even an experienced breeder of Australian finches must ensure that sufficient housing is available for any youngsters about to be bred. If space is limited, then only keep the number of breeding pairs for whose chicks accommodation is available. To overcrowd young birds because you are short of space could mean that heavy losses will occur, thus undoing all the work you have put in over the year.

Australian finches can be housed in aviaries, cages, or indoor flights. Read the advice given under each separate heading and decide which type of accommodation suits you best. If space allows, then you may decide to combine all three modes of housing. The area or country in which you live should also be taken into account when deciding how you intend to house your birds. In the warmer areas of Australia and the United States, aviaries are the norm, whereas in the United Kingdom and on the continent of Europe cages and/or indoor flights are favored, especially for those species which require a fairly warm environment. More detailed information on housing will be found under AVIARIES, BIRDROOMS, CAGES, and INDOOR FLIGHTS. Under each individual species heading, details will be found on the housing considered most suitable for that particular species.

AVIARIES
Much interest and enjoyment can be obtained from birds housed in aviaries, as their owner is then able to observe much of their natural behavior, something denied to those who keep their birds solely in cages.

An aviary usually consists of an all-wire flight attached to a wooden or brick shelter. Planning permission is usually required for such a construction and it would be prudent to approach your local officials before erecting such accommodation.

The site of the aviary should be selected with care; it should not be sited near to trees or fences as these will make it easy for cats to get onto the roof of the shelter and/or the flight. If trees overhang the aviary, wild birds may perch in the branches and their droppings

An aviary with removable, sliding plastic windows. Full use has been made of growing plants, thus providing an ideal environment for Australian finches. Note the separate doors leading to the safety porch.

could spread disease. Leaves falling on the aviary roof could also create problems.

The site chosen should also avoid any obvious source of disturbance such as children's swings, clotheslines, etc. Other factors which need to be considered are easy access and space sufficient to extend the aviary should you wish to do so at some future date. If protection from prevailing winds, by means of brick walls or stout fencing, is already available in the immediate area, then so much the better. A clear space of at least 90 cm (3 ft) around the perimeter of the aviary is advisable, thus making the checking and maintenance of the structure easier.

The size of the aviary

In temperate zones, the number of birds kept in such a structure should be limited to however many can safely be housed in the shelter without overcrowding, as in inclement weather conditions, it may prove necessary to confine the birds to the shelter. It is difficult to give an exact figure as to the number of birds that can safely be housed in an aviary without overcrowding as the compatibility of the species concerned needs to be taken into account (see COMPATIBILITY). I would suggest, therefore, that at least 1 sq m (1 sq yd) of floor space be allowed for each breeding pair. Obviously, if only resting adults or youngsters are housed in the aviary, then more birds could be accommodated than is suggested for breeding pairs.

In the latter case, the availability of roosting perches is the deciding factor. Noncontact birds (i.e., those species which do not roost close together, such as Gouldian Finches) would require approximately 15 cm (6 in) of roosting perch each. This would mean that in a shelter measuring 1.8 m by 90 cm (6 × 3 ft), if a single roosting perch was placed along one side of the 90-cm length, then approximately six non-breeding birds could be housed in the aviary. However, by placing the perch the other way, or by adding two perches (one on each side of the shelter), the capacity would be greater.

It must be emphasized, however, that the numbers mentioned are only meant as a guide. When the birds are first introduced into the aviary, careful observations should be maintained. This is especially important during the evenings, when the birds are going to roost, to ensure that serious bickering does not occur.

The size of the flight area need only be confined to the amount of space available. However, it must be remembered that no matter how large the flight, the number of birds kept must relate to the actual size of the *shelter*. Supports for the flight can be of timber, metal, or

brick, although the latter two materials could prove expensive. The ideal covering for the flight is welded mesh netting, sold under various trade names. If possible, heavy-gauge wire should be used. Although it may be more expensive than the finer gauge, it will last considerably longer and because of this will prove to be more economical over the years. Either 9 mm (³⁄₈ in)-square or 9 mm × 2.5 cm (³⁄₈ × 1 in) mesh is suitable; it is possible, however, that mice may enter a flight made of 9 mm × 2.5 cm mesh, and I would therefore recommend 9 mm square as a better size.

A commercially built aviary may have its wooden structure already

An outdoor aviary, with a Georgian wired glass roof, is connected to an indoor flight used for housing and breeding Diamond Firetails.

weatherproofed. If it is not, then you should apply a good-quality protective sealer (which is nonpoisonous) and ensure that this is completely dry before introducing birds into the aviary. Creosote is one of the sealants most often used, however it can take an extraordinary length of time to dry out completely, especially if applied during cold, damp weather. Also, if creosote comes into contact with plants, it may kill them, or at least severely burn their leaves. Because of this, I prefer to use one of the protective sealants recommended for fencing. These are not only obtainable in various colors, but many are completely harmless to plant life. A further point in their favor is that they dry quickly.

It is doubtful if a commercially built aviary will have the wire mesh already treated, and a coat of asphalt paint should be applied (a paint roller being the easiest tool to use) well before the birds are introduced. This will not only help to preserve the wire mesh but will also make it more attractive to the eye and enable the birds to be viewed more easily.

As long as a warm, brightly lit shelter is available, the flight area can be open to the elements. However, you may prefer to partially enclose the flight. This would certainly prove beneficial if some of the birds nested in the flight. Sudden heavy downpours of rain are one of the most common causes of losses in chicks, due to them either being washed out of the nest or, if they have recently fledged, becoming saturated with rain water, thus causing them to become chilled. As a temporary measure, strong polyethylene sheeting could be attached to the roof of the flight. The polyethylene must be firmly battened down, as any left to flap in the wind would no doubt cause stress to the birds. If you decide to cover the flight partially on a permanent basis, clear plastic, sheeting would prove the most suitable material to use.

The floor

The floor of the flight can be grassed over, or, if you prefer, covered with small stone chips. Alternatively, concrete could be laid. A grass-covered area would certainly be attractive. If the aviary is to be used during the summer months only, grass could prove ideal as during the period when the aviary was unoccupied, any areas which had become bare would have the opportunity to regrow. However, for an aviary which is in constant use, I would suggest that a covering of stone chips (approximately 15 cm/6 in in depth) would be more suitable. The chips could then be hosed down regularly, as, indeed, could a concrete base.

If you intend to house a mixed collection of Australian finches in the aviary (see individual species and/or COMPATIBILITY for information on those birds most suitable for a mixed collection), then it would be preferable to plant out the flight with small nonpoisonous bushes and creepers, thus enabling the more retiring species to hide away if need be (see PLANTS FOR AVIARIES).

A planted aviary can look most attractive. If a floor of stone chips or concrete is used, the area could still be planted out, but the bushes or shrubs would then, of course, have to be housed in containers. Even so, an attractive layout can still be created, especially if the tubs are sunk into the gravel or chips, thus giving the impression that the plants are actually growing in the ground rather than in containers. An advantage of this particular system is that container-grown plants can be interchanged from time to time, so that any that become partly denuded of leaves or heavily soiled with droppings can be replaced and allowed to recover before being used again in the aviary.

The shelter

As already mentioned, the size of the actual shelter will determine the number of birds that can be housed in the aviary. The shelter must prove attractive to the inmates, thus ensuring that they use it regularly. This is especially important during inclement weather conditions. A brick shelter could be utilized, but unless you already have an existing building which could be converted, the initial costs may prove a deterrent. An existing garden shed could be used, but it would need to have plenty of window space, as a dark shelter would deter birds from entering.

Whether you use an existing shed or build a specially designed shelter, both should be treated with weatherproofing before birds are introduced. The inside walls and ceiling should be lined with insulation boards and all windows should be double-glazed, thus saving considerably on heating costs. Roosting perches should be fixed as high as possible and nest boxes can be hung along the walls in the hope that they will encourage the inmates to nest in the shelter rather than in the outside flight.

If the flight is planted, certain species of birds will no doubt prefer to build nests in the bushes or shrubs, but if the majority of the birds can be persuaded to nest in the shelter, then so much the better, as stricter control can then be maintained over them.

Heating

If the birds are species which are considered suitable for housing in the aviary all year round, rather than for the warmer months only, then some form of heating will have to be supplied. I consider the most suitable to be a good quality electric fan-heater, which is run in conjunction with a reliable thermostat. This type of heater must be located in an area to which the birds are unable to gain access, otherwise the fan heater would soon become soiled with droppings and seed husks and, because of this, cease to function correctly. If it is not possible to locate the heater in an area where it will not become fouled, you will have no option but to install tubular heaters. Such heaters give off far less heat than a fan heater and you may thus be limited in the species which can be kept by the temperature levels which this form of heating provides (see TEMPERATURE and ELECTRICAL INSTALLATION).

Access

Food and water should always be placed in the shelter rather than in the outside flight. I would suggest that two access holes be provided to enable the birds to move freely to and from the shelter and flight. If only one access hole is made, a dominant bird may stand guard over the hole, refusing entry or exit to other inmates. Perches should be placed near the access holes, both in the shelter and in the flight, to encourage free movement between both areas. A sliding cover, which can be operated from the outside of the aviary, should be fitted to the access holes, thus allowing either section to be closed off without the keeper having to enter the aviary.

It is also advantageous if a connecting door to the flight is built into the shelter to allow the owner easy access. If such a door is included, then only one safety door would be required, this being attached either to the flight or to the shelter. If there is no connecting door between the shelter and flight, then two safety doors would be required, one attached to the shelter and the other to the flight. Without such a door or doors, losses will almost certainly occur through birds escaping when their owner enters the aviary.

B

BANDED FINCH (see BICHENO FINCH)

BATHING
Australian finches are usually keen to bathe although certain species may refrain from doing so when in heavy molt.

For those housed in aviaries or large indoor flights, a fairly large shallow dish, no more than 4 cm (1½ in) in depth, should be kept in the enclosure at all times. The bath will require cleaning and replenishing each day, preferably in the early morning. For caged birds, I provide a bath every other day, as to leave one permanently in the cage would mean that the cage floor would be continually damp. The ideal receptacle is a 12-cm (5 in) plastic flowerpot saucer. This can be placed in the cage first thing in the morning, to one side of the cage, well away from perches and food containers. The saucer should, if possible, be removed within an hour or so, thoroughly

A sophisticated drip-fed bath, ensuring a continuous supply of fresh bathing water. One possible drawback is the time that must be spent in cleaning it.

washed and dried and stacked, ready again for use.

When a number of birds are housed in a flight cage (such as resting adults or weaned youngsters), the area where the bath is placed can become extremely damp and this could eventually prove damaging to a cage made of wood. To avoid this, self-adhesive vinyl should be laid on the area where the bathing saucers are placed, thus preventing water seeping into the floor of the cage.

Many bird keepers use plastic clip-on baths of the type manufactured for pet birds. These can be hung on the cage front over the door. However, with certain species, such as Bicheno Finches, I am wary of such baths, as newly fledged chicks could enter the bath and fail to find their way out before becoming saturated with water. In such a condition they could soon become chilled and, if not found in time, they might die.

BEAUTIFUL FIRETAIL (*Emblema bella*)
The adult cock, from forehead to lower back, wings and lower tail, is olive-brown with fine blackish barring; the rump, upper-tail coverts, and basal edges of the tail are bright crimson; the lores and through the eye, the center of the abdomen and the under-tail coverts are black with the remainder of the underparts light gray, finely barred with black. The beak is red; the eye-ring pale blue. Hens resemble the cock but have the abdomen barred, not black. The total length is 115–120 mm (4½–4¾ in).

The Beautiful Firetail is one of the most secretive of the Australian finches. Tasmania is its main stronghold, in fact it is the only Australian finch native to this state. On the Australian mainland it is also found along the coast of New South Wales, from the Hunter River south to coastal Victoria and west to southeastern South Australia.

Its preferred habitat is dense vegetation in wet heathland areas, heavily timbered woodland, and densely covered gullies in mountainous areas.

No longer known to aviculture outside Australia, the Beautiful Firetail can only be kept in captivity in its country of origin if a special permit is obtained. It has been bred in captivity but is, without doubt, an extremely difficult species to keep alive, let alone breed. It is doubtful if it will ever become established in aviaries even in Australia.

BENGALESE FINCH (SOCIETY FINCH)

At one time this bird, known in North America as the Society Finch and in Britain and other English-speaking areas as the Bengalese, was considered to be a fertile hybrid. Various species have been suggested as possible ancestors, including Spice Birds and Silverbills. Even today, one sometimes hears this theory expressed. However, it is now established that the Society is a domesticated form of the Striated Finch (*Lonchura striata*).

The Australian finch enthusiast has much to thank the Society Finch for, as without its superb fostering abilities, the number of Australian finch species available today would be far less than it is.

Here the Society Finch will only be considered as a foster parent for Australian finch chicks (see FOSTERING). It should be mentioned, however, that Society Finches are kept by many people as exhibition birds, having their own society and exhibition standards.

If you wish to keep Society Finches as fosters, then they should be from a good strain of known fosters. Not all Society Finches make good foster parents and any which fail to rear successfully

should be discarded. On no account should they be allowed to breed themselves, as the progeny from such pairs would probably prove to be poor fosters also.

A good strain of fosters are well worth the care and attention lavished upon them. Numerous mutations are available; all are suitable as fosters. Birds used as fosters must be housed in cages and the diet supplied should be as prescribed for Australian finches, minus the charcoal granules.

A great advantage with Society Finches is that no matter what stage their breeding cycle has reached, it is relatively simple to persuade them to take on eggs or young. It is preferable for eggs or chicks to be fostered to a pair whose breeding cycle is close to that of the parent Australian finch pair, but I do not find this a critical point. While I remove the nest box from certain species of Australian finch (see NEST BOXES) when their chicks are approximately one month old, I always leave the box with Societys, as taking it away may cause stress. Invariably, the Societys will produce a further clutch of eggs by the time their foster chicks are ready to be weaned, but they are such accommodating birds that, after the Australian finch chicks have been removed, the nest box can be thoroughly cleaned, fresh hay added, and the eggs already laid can be returned to the cleaned nest. The Societys will then continue to incubate, regardless of the disruption.

A Dilute Chocolate and White Society (Bengalese) Finch. All mutations are suitable as fosters for Australian finches.

A breeder may not wish to give over valuable space to birds used solely for fostering, so once a strain of self-rearing Australian finch species has been developed, two or three pairs of Society Finches are all that would be required for a stud of approximately ten breeding pairs. If the Societys are not required for fostering, then they can be allowed to rear young of their own, as good quality Society Finches, which are known to be from a good fostering strain, are always in demand.

BICHENO FINCH (*Poephila bichenovii*) (color photos on pages 118–9, 122)

Two subspecies of the Bicheno Finch are recognized, *P. b. bichenovii*, which has a white rump, and *P. b. annulosa*, which has a black rump. The former is found in eastern Australia, while the Black-rumped race is found in the Top End and Kimberley regions. The two interbreed in a broad area south of the Gulf of Carpentaria. The species' range has expanded toward the coast in lower eastern Queensland and the southeast regions. It has also expanded southward into the Murray-Darling region. In the wild, the Bicheno lives in close-knit groups of four to twenty birds. It is always near water, usually in woodland with a grassy undergrowth, but can also be found in acacia scrub and on cultivated land such as parks and gardens.

The White-rumped race is well known wherever Australian finches are kept, but the Black-rumped race has been virtually unknown and may only be available in small numbers in Europe. Until recently, numbers were fairly low in the United States and the United Kingdom also, but over the past three or four years more interest has been taken in preserving the Black-rumped race and at the time of writing reasonable numbers are being produced, so that it now appears to be secure.

In Australia the species is usually referred to as the Double-bar Finch. Other names include Banded Finch (for the White-rumped race) and Ringed Finch (for the Black-rumped). It is also called the Owl Finch, especially in the USA where only this name appears to be used.

The Bicheno is one of the smallest of the Australian finches, its overall size being approximately 101 mm (4 in). The upperparts are pale grayish-brown, finely barred with dark brown. The lower rump and upper-tail coverts are white (or black in the Black-rumped race); the tail is dark brown. The secondaries and greater wing coverts are blackish, barred with white. The face, including the area above the eyes and ear coverts, is silvery-white, encircled by a narrow

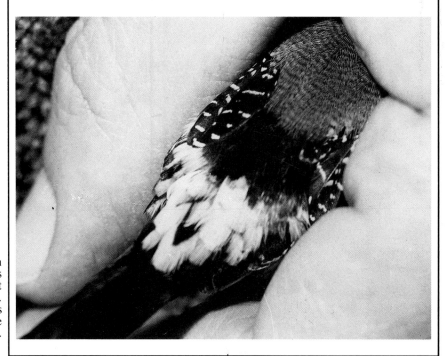

A Bicheno Finch which is White-rumped split for Black-rumped. In genetic terms this would be written WR/br.

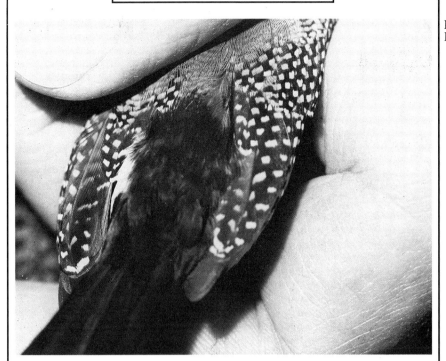

Bicheno Finch.
Black-rumped race.

black band running from the forehead, around the cheeks and across to divide the throat from the breast. The breast is also silvery-white, sharply divided by another black band across the lower breast. The remainder of the underparts is creamy white, except for the under-tail coverts which are black. The beak is grayish-blue. The sexes are similar (see MONOMORPHIC SPECIES).

If the Bicheno Finch is housed in an aviary, then a heated shelter must be provided. In the more temperate areas of the world, aviary birds should, if possible, be persuaded to nest in the shelter, as inclement weather conditions could cause serious losses among chicks being reared in outside flights, especially if sudden heavy downpours of rain were to occur shortly after the youngsters have left the nest. Without any form of shelter, the young birds could become saturated with rain and, if unable to dry out fairly quickly,

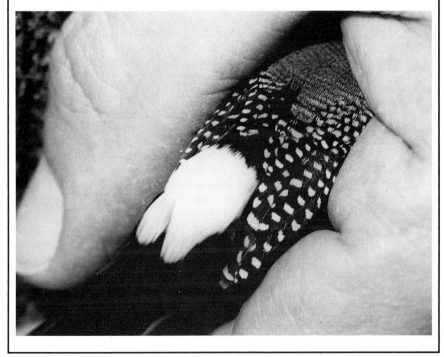

Bicheno Finch.
White-rumped
race.

they would soon become chilled.

Bicheno Finches will mix well with other species of a similar size and temperament, but Zebra Finches should never be included in the same aviary, as the species are similar in many ways and hybridization may occur. For the same reason, Zebra Finches should never be used to foster deserted eggs or young from Bichenos as, in all probability, the young would become imprinted on the Zebra Finch fosters.

Due to the sexes being almost identical, one of the main problems experienced by potential breeders of the Bicheno has been the difficulty of obtaining true pairs. It is often suggested that individuals with wide chest-bars and brighter face masks and chests are invariably cocks. I have also seen it stated that the black feathers immediately above the beak are wider and of a deeper color in the cock. Such observations no doubt prove correct in certain cases, but what does one do when confronted with a poorly marked cock or an exceptionally well-marked hen?

In fact, the only reliable method is to use the song as an indication of sex. For this method, see SEXING.

Bichenos can be used for breeding from approximately nine months of age. They will have attained full adult plumage long before this; indeed the majority of youngsters molt into adult plumage within ten weeks of hatching. However, if these are compared with birds of nine months or more, it will be seen that the younger birds are smaller in size. If used too soon for breeding, hens often experience problems with egg-binding, due to attempting to lay eggs before they are fully mature (see EGG-BINDING). If you are not entirely sure of the age of a hen, then rather than putting her down to breed when there is a possibility she is too young, house her with other hens and, eventually, if in breeding condition, she will begin to lay eggs — a sure sign that she is old enough to breed.

A clutch usually consists of between four to six eggs. Incubation does not begin in earnest until the third or fourth egg is laid. Both parent birds take turns in incubating and both remain on the nest overnight. The young hatch after approximately 12 days. When the chicks are seven days old, the parent birds will brood only spasmodically, and by the time the chicks have reached nine days of age, brooding ceases altogether, although the parent birds will continue to sleep on the nest during the night. Chicks begin to leave the nest at approximately 26 days of age. At around this age they can prove somewhat delicate and any which appear to be unable to return to the nest should be gently caught up and placed back in the nest. As the chicks become more mature, they will spend longer periods away from the nest but will always return to roost. They can be removed from their parents at between five to six weeks of age. If left longer, the parent birds may attack them.

As mentioned earlier, there are two subspecies, one with a white rump, the other with a rump which is black. In the wild, where the two races overlap, they frequently interbreed. Due, no doubt, to the White-rumped race being dominant to the Black-rumped (see GENETICS), numbers of the latter became very low and only in recent times have sufficient enthusiasts taken up the breeding of the Black-rumped Bicheno to ensure its availability for future aviculturists.

Being dominant, if a *pure* White-rumped is mated to a Black-rumped, the resulting young will be visual White-rumped split for Black-rumped. If these split birds are mated to a Black-rumped, then approximately 50 percent Black-rumped and 50 percent visual White-rumped split for Black-rumped will be produced. As the Bicheno does not appear to follow the usual pattern of inheritance, it is possible to identify certain split birds by the black feathers or markings on an otherwise white rump. This means that if one has two split birds only, they can be mated together (something not recommended for most mutations) as not only will Black-rumped birds be produced (approximately 25 percent), but splits will also appear (approximately 50 percent), as will pure White-rumped (approximately 25 percent). Normally it would be impossible to identify the split birds from such a mating, but as some will almost certainly have black-and-white rumps, these alone could be classed as split birds, with those showing only white on the rump being classed as White-rumped birds (even though a certain percentage would be split birds). (See GENETICS.)

BIRDROOMS

A birdroom is usually a building, no matter how large or small, which is fitted out with cages and/or flights. Obviously the smaller the birdroom, the fewer breeding pairs you can keep. However, no matter what the size, if successful breeding is to be accomplished, then certain rules should be adhered to.

An outside birdroom should be well insulated and the windows should be double-glazed, thus saving considerably on heating costs. An electricity supply must be installed, as no matter what species is kept, heating will be required during the colder months of the year. Lighting will also need to be installed. Fluorescent tubes fitted to the ceiling of the birdroom are to be preferred, as not only are they economical to run, they also give off a superior light compared with ordinary light bulbs, and tend to throw less shadow into the cages. (See ELECTRICAL INSTALLATION.)

If a spare room is available in your own house, it could be converted into an ideal birdroom. There would, of course, be no need to insulate the walls, but it would be prudent to double-glaze the windows.

Cleanliness is most important and the floor of the birdroom may be easily cleaned if a good-quality vinyl floor covering is laid. This would be almost essential if a room in your own house is used, but even an outside birdroom can look far more attractive if the floor is covered. Good-quality vinyl will last for years; it should be cleaned regularly, using warm water with a small amount of disinfectant.

The birdroom must be bright and airy; my own birdroom has the ceiling painted white and the walls pale green. If a good-quality silk vinyl emulsion is used, the walls and ceiling can easily be wiped down periodically and should only require repainting every two or three years.

Someone starting from scratch should plan the layout of the birdroom in detail before purchasing or making cages or flights. These can then be made so as to utilize all available space to the best advantage.

A bright, airy, well-planned birdroom is a delight to work in and, if a little thought is given to the actual layout, even a small garden shed can be adequately adapted to house a few breeding pairs.

BLACK-THROATED FINCH
(*Poephila cincta*) (color photos on pages 90–91)

The approximate overall length is 101 mm (4 in). The crown and nape are gray; the hindneck and upper portion of the back are cinnamon-brown, with the lower back and wings brown. The rump is black as are the tail feathers. The upper-tail coverts are white. The forehead, ear coverts, and cheeks are whitish-gray; the lores and throat are black, with the remainder of the underparts cinnamon, except for the abdomen and under-tail coverts, which are white. There is also a large black patch on the lower flanks. The beak is black. The sexes are similar (see MONOMORPHIC SPECIES).

The favored habitat is open, lightly wooded savannah grassland. This species lives in loose, sedentary flocks of up to 30 birds.

I had difficulty in knowing just what common name to use as a heading for this species. The correct name (as used by ornithologists) is Black-throated Finch. This is also the name used by aviculturists in Australia. However, in the USA, the UK, and on the continent of Europe the species has always been referred to by aviculturists as the Parson Finch.

At present there is considerable debate as to the number of different subspecies. What we term a Parson Finch was at one time given subspecies status (*P. c. vinotinctus*), but is now classed as a light form of *P. c. cincta*. In captivity, the light form is bred in substantial numbers and is certainly secure. In the wild, however, it is declining rapidly.

Other forms of the Black-throated Finch are discussed under DIGGLES FINCH.

Gouldian Finches (1)

Red-headed Gouldian Finch (cock). This head color is dominant to both the Black- and the Orange-headed. This means that if a *pure* Red-headed is mated to either of the other head colors, all progeny will have red heads. Due, no doubt, to being dominant, the Red-headed is the head color most often seen in captive-bred birds.

A Gouldian Finch in immature plumage. Note the light-reflecting tubercles on the sides of the face (near the beak). These tubercles disappear a few weeks after fledging.

A pair of Black-headed Gouldian Finches. The hen is on the left.

In the wild, this head color is reported to outnumber the Red-headed form by three to one. This is surprising, as the latter is dominant to the Black-headed.

The majority of Black-headed Gouldian Finches have good overall depth of color and, because of this, make excellent exhibition birds.

Orange-headed Gouldian Finch pair – Yellow (or Yellow-backed) mutation. The hen is on the left.

This is one of the more recent mutations and, as yet, the actual genetic make-up is not fully understood. As can be seen, the head color in this mutation is on a par with that of a normal Orange-headed; the same applies to the Red-headed. However, as this mutation does not manufacture the black pigment, melanin, in the Black-headed form the head is either pale yellowish-gray or pale slate-gray.

The light form is found in central and southern Queensland, south of latitude 17 degrees south from Townsville to Roma. A Chocolate form is found in northern New South Wales and southern Queensland, near the state border. It is also found in small areas west of the Great Dividing Range. In the wild, the Chocolate race is very rare and, as mentioned earlier, it appears that the light race is also on the decline.

The Black-throated Finch is a most attractive species which can be housed and bred successfully in a cage, an aviary, or an indoor flight. It will breed successfully in the colony system, but under such conditions there may be problems with certain individuals becoming overly aggressive toward others of their kind. In a mixed collection, two or three pairs could be housed with other species of a similar size (except for Masked, Long-tailed, and Heck's Grassfinches with which they would, no doubt, hybridize), but the Black-throated would need to be watched carefully to ensure they did not interfere with the nesting arrangements of the other species. Also, the numbers of Black-throated would have to be kept at a reasonable level (removing young as they became independent would be the easiest method), otherwise they may 'gang up' on the other inmates, with disastrous results.

Probably the most suitable way in which to breed this finch is to house individual pairs in small flights or roomy cages. Sexing can prove difficult, especially for someone new to the species. Cocks supposedly have a larger and wider black throat patch than the hens, and the black lores and flank stripes are also wider in most cock birds. A more reliable method is to sex the birds by the song of the cock (see SEXING).

The average clutch size is between five and seven eggs and incubation does not usually commence until the full clutch is laid. Both birds take turns in incubating but it is usually the hen which sits during the night. The incubation period is normally between 12 to 14 days and the parent birds cease to brood when the chicks are some ten days of age. They will, however, return to the nest for the night. The young

fledge at approximately 22 days and become independent at approximately five to six weeks. Immature birds are similar in appearance to the adults but have less well-defined markings and smaller throat patches.

The Chocolate form (given the name Chocolate Diggles in Australia) has the lower breast and abdomen reddish-chocolate-brown rather than the light cinnamon-brown of the 'Normal' Black-throated Finch. The Chocolate form is not only extremely rare in the wild, it is also rare in aviculture, even in its country of origin. It is, however, increasing steadily in Australian aviaries but is still extremely rare in the United States, Central Europe and the United Kingdom.

As with the Heck's Grassfinch, four mutations are available in the Black-throated. The Fawn is widely bred and, pricewise, costs no more than the Normal phase. Pied specimens are somewhat rare and command the highest figure of all the mutations. Creams (which are extremely attractive) and Whites are fairly numerous and will, no doubt, eventually cost no more to purchase than a good class Normal.

Whether or not all the above mutations came directly from Black-throated Finches, I cannot say. What is certain is that mutation Heck's Grassfinches have most certainly been mated to Black-throated, as many of the supposedly 'pure' mutation Black-throated have Heck's blood in their veins, obvious from the reddish color of the beaks of some individuals. This practice is to be abhorred and is, I hope, no longer resorted to. There is certainly little need to produce these 'mongrel'-type birds, as there are sufficient numbers in all of the mutations for them to be secure in aviculture without having to resort to crossmating species.

BLUE-FACED PARROT FINCH (*Erythrura trichroa*) (color photos on page 115)
The overall size is approximately 121 mm (4¾ in). The general color of the upper parts is a rich grass-green. The lores, forehead, superciliary, cheeks, and ear coverts are blue; the upper-tail coverts are crimson; the tail is brown edged with crimson. The

Blue-faced Parrot Finch.

underparts are light grass-green, tinged with golden-olive on the thighs. The beak is black. The sexes are similar (see MONOMORPHIC SPECIES).

This species is restricted to small areas of rain forest along the coastal plains and foothills of northeastern Queensland. It is widely distributed in New Guinea and can also be found in the Celebes, the Moluccas, the Bismark Archipelago, the Solomons, the Pellew Islands, the Carolines, the New Hebrides, and the Loyalty Islands. It prefers dense growth adjacent to rain forest and mangroves, but may also be found near human settlements.

The Blue-faced is the only parrot finch found in Australia; it is also the one most commonly found in aviculture. Due to its active nature, it is usually considered to be more suited to an aviary than a cage. However, a fair number are cage-bred each year. Due to their robust mating habits (the cock bird often takes hold of the hen's head feathers, and sometimes her body feathers also, when copulation is about to take place), the hen of a pair which is caged can become

heavily plucked. By the end of the breeding season she may look a somewhat sorry sight.

Sexing can be a problem, especially if one is confronted with well-colored hens and poorly colored cock birds. Well-colored cocks usually have a brighter, deeper face mask, while the actual body color is normally a more brilliant grass-green. As with many monomorphic species, it is preferable, if guaranteed true pairs are not available, to purchase a number of birds rather than just two. There is then a good possibility that at least one pair will be forthcoming.

Blue-faced are a hardy species and it is possible to house them in an aviary all year round as long as they have access to a heated shelter. They should be discouraged from breeding during the colder months unless they can be persuaded to use nest boxes placed in the heated shelter. As I have mentioned elsewhere (see CLOSED-BANDS), if a species can be persuaded always to use nest boxes rather than building a nest in the aviary flight, then it is much easier to keep a check on the nest and to

Gouldian Finches (2)

Red-headed Gouldian Finch (cock) – White-breasted mutation. This is a good example of the White-breasted mutation. Note the deep red head, pure white breast and well colored lower breast and abdomen.

The White-breasted first appeared in Australia in 1954 and in South Africa in the late 1950s. Although recessive to the Normal, it is firmly established and large numbers are bred each year.

Black-headed Gouldian Finch (cock) – White-breasted mutation. A fine example of the mutation. The overall color is excellent and the well-developed tail wires (often lacking in White-breasted birds) add greatly to the elegance of the bird.

closed-band the chicks. If the parrot finches do insist on building their own nests in the outside flight, then as long as weather conditions are fairly warm, chicks will no doubt be reared to maturity, although whether or not you will still be able to fit the chicks with closed-bands is debatable.

The clutch usually consists of between four and six eggs and incubation lasts from 12 to 14 days. The chicks leave the nest at approximately 21 days after hatching and are dull green in color. At approximately eight weeks of age, they begin to molt into adult plumage and are often sexually mature by the time they are five months of age. They should not, however, be allowed to breed at such an early age but should be held in a communal flight or large flight cage until they are at least nine to ten months of age,

after which they can, if in breeding condition, be paired up and placed in their breeding quarters.

As well as the usual seeds recommended for Australian finches, Blue-faced Parrot Finches will, when they have young in the nest, take large quantities of live food (see LIVE FOOD). A good proprietary brand of soft food (see SOFT FOOD) should also be provided on a regular basis. Certain soft fruits may also be sampled, such as ripe pear or soft apple.

Only one mutation has so far occurred in the Blue-faced, namely the Lutino. The overall color is yellow (birds can be found in varying shades from deep yellow to pale lemon), with the face mask, flights, and tail white and the rump red (paler than in the Normal bird). The beak is also white. When the Lutino first appeared in the United Kingdom, the price asked was in the region of £250 a

Species	Clutch Size	Incubation Period (days)	Fledging Time (days)
Beautiful Firetail	4–5	13–15	21–25
Bicheno Finch	4–6	12–14	20–23
Black-throated Finch	5–7	12–14	21–23
Blue-faced Parrot Finch	4–6	12–14	21–22
Chestnut-breasted Finch	4–6	12–14	21–22
Crimson Finch	4–8	13–14	20–21
Diamond Firetail	4–8	12–15	23–26
Gouldian Finch	4–8	14–15	21–25
Long-tailed Grassfinch	4–6	12–14	21–24
Masked Grassfinch	4–6	13–15	20–23
Painted Firetail	3–5	13–14	23–26
Pictorella Finch	4–6	12–14	21–24
Plum-headed Finch	4–7	12–14	19–21
Red-browed Finch	4–6	13–14	17–21
Red-eared Firetail	4–6	12–14	21–24
Star Finch	4–7	12–15	17–21
Yellow-rumped Finch	4–5	12–14	21–22

pair. However, as the number of Lutinos increased, so the price dropped, and now specimens can be purchased for a much more reasonable figure.

Attempts have been made to produce a sea-green mutation (also a pied), as found in the Red-headed Parrot Finch (*E. psittacae*), by pairing examples of the latter with Blue-faced. However, one should be wary of purchasing these 'mongrel' birds as it would prove extremely difficult to produce 'pure' Blue-faced chicks from such birds.

BLOOD FINCH (see CRIMSON FINCH)

BREEDING
The ultimate aim of anyone keeping Australian finches is to breed from them. In 1960 Australia placed a ban on all exportation of its fauna and all Australian finches held outside of Australia have come from stock already held when the ban came into operation. That many of the species referred to in this book are now virtually domesticated (see DOMESTICATION) is due to the breeding efforts of the many Australian-finch enthusiasts throughout the world. Certain species, due to the difficulties experienced when attempting to breed from them, are rarely seen in captivity, even in their country of origin. However, due to their popularity, many species are well established in our cages and aviaries and will no doubt remain so.

See under the individual species headings for details of individual breeding requirements.

BREEDING DATA
The chart on the left gives an at-a-glance guide to the clutch size, incubation period, and fledging times of Australian finches.

CAGES
The majority of Australian finches are ideally suited to cage-breeding and many enthusiasts, even in countries where the weather conditions allow stock to be housed permanently in aviaries, still prefer to cage-breed their birds, as much stricter control can thus be maintained. Nowadays many enthusiasts line- or inbreed their birds (see LINEBREEDING and INBREEDING), while others are interested in perpetuating the large number of mutations available (see GENETICS). For such people, cage-breeding is a must.

Fairly recently, attempts were made to breed Australian finches in all-wire cages. From the reports I have read, these cages have proved unsuitable, mainly because the inmates had no sense of security. I am surprised that all-wire cages were ever considered suitable accommodation, as even a complete beginner must be encouraged to use what are usually referred to as 'box cages' if successful breeding is to be attempted. (A box cage is an all-wood cage with a wire front.)

I consider the minimum size of breeding cage suitable for Australian finches to be 91 × 41 × 41 cm (36 × 16 × 16 in). If your stock is housed permanently in cages, then it is preferable to have cages of at least 1.8 m (6 ft) in length. These can be fitted with a removable divider (usually made of plywood) and during the breeding season a breeding pair can be housed in each section. The divider can be removed after the breeding season and the cage will then prove ideal for growing young birds or for resting adults. I would suggest that no more than ten birds be housed in a cage of this size.

The insides of the cage should be painted, using a good-quality vinyl emulsion. I use pale green rather than white, as I feel this color is more restful for the birds. Cage fronts can be either of bars or welded mesh, the latter having a mesh of no more than 9 mm × 2.5

Gouldian Finches (3)

Red-headed Gouldian Finch (cock) – White-breasted mutation. Note the pearly white beak with a reddish tip, denoting that the bird is in breeding condition. This bird has rather poor head coloring, i.e., the red is not as vivid as it should be. This is a fault seen nowadays in many Red-headed birds, both in Normals and White-breasteds.

Red-headed Gouldian Finch (hen) – White-breasted mutation. Note the blackish-colored beak which denotes that the bird is in breeding condition. Although it is usual for hen Gouldian Finches in breeding condition to have a blackish-colored beak, this is not always the case and hens may successfully go to nest and rear young without any color change in their beaks. More obvious signs are when a hen can be seen to become 'heavy,' with a pronounced rise to the rump and the tail held in a downwards position. Also, hens in breeding condition will continually nest call.

Orange-headed Gouldian Finch (cock).

Often given the name Yellow-headed, this head color is rare in the wild and is said to occur in no more than approximately one per five to ten thousand birds. The Orange-headed is well established in aviculture and, although not as commonly available as the Red-headed form, large numbers are bred each year.

One of a block of breeding cages used by the author.

cm (⅜ × 1 in). Bar fronts should have a space of no more than 9 mm between each bar. I prefer two doors to be incorporated into the cage front, both being at least 15 cm (6 in) square. One of the doors should be situated in the center of the cage front, with the bottom of the door resting on the bottom spar. The other door should be situated in the extreme top lefthand corner for the lefthand cage and in the righthand corner for the righthand cage. This allows easy access to the nest box which, in my cages, is hung on the solid side wall of the cage (see NEST BOXES).

To make the cage fronts more attractive to the eye and to enable the birds to be seen more easily, it is a good idea to paint the wire fronts black. I use black emulsion, which can be applied either with a roller or a paint brush. This task is made easier if the cage front is placed on a flat surface on which several layers of clean newspaper have first been laid. The cage front can then be placed on the newspaper and the emulsion paint applied carefully, ensuring that all parts of the front are covered. After this, the front should be propped up against a clean surface until dry. I have read that blackboard paint is excellent and can prove to be more hard wearing than emulsion. Gloss paint is not recommended as it would need to be stripped each year before a new

coat could be added — a most time-consuming and laborious task.

I do not have dropping trays in my cages as I prefer to use newspaper as a floor covering. A removable 25 mm (1 in) wooden bar is fitted to the front of each cage, allowing the easy removal of soiled newspaper during the cleaning-out process (see FLOOR COVERING).

It should be remembered that adequate accommodation will be required for any young birds bred, and a number of empty cages should be reserved in the hope that these will eventually be filled with healthy young birds!

Cages require renovating on a regular basis and the ideal time to do this is when adult pairs have been split up and surplus young have been sold. Empty cages can then be thoroughly washed, repaired if need be, and then repainted.

CATCHING
It is inevitable that, from time to time, you will have to catch birds for some reason. If the birds are housed in an aviary, then the tool to use is a good-quality hand net with a padded rim. Catching birds, especially from an aviary, is distressing for both the keeper and the birds, and therefore you should only catch your birds when it is absolutely necessary.

Even an experienced person would find it difficult to catch birds in a large aviary (or indoor flight) and at such times a baited trap may prove less distressing not only for the birds but for their owner also. A funnel-type trap may prove suitable, i.e., an all-wire cage, entry to which is provided by a small hole in one side of the cage, to which has been added a funnel-like entrance made of wire mesh. If the trap is baited with seed, and all food is removed from the aviary, the bird may eventually enter the trap by the entrance funnel. As the exit hole is smaller in diameter than the entrance hole, the bird will be unable to escape.

Another type of trap is one which has a pressure-sensitive perch attached to a sliding door. The bird enters the trap and as it lands on the perch the perch moves downward, thus closing the trap door. Both types of traps are simple to make, but you may have to wait some time for the particular bird or birds you wish to catch to enter the cage.

Another method is to use an all-wire trap-cage which has the door propped open with a piece of wood (or something similar) to which is attached a length of strong black thread. The thread is passed through the aviary wire and reeled out until it is far enough away for a person to hold the thread and be able to observe the birds without them being aware of this fact. The person holding the thread waits until the bird he or she wishes to catch enters the trap. Then, with a swift tug on the thread, the door prop is released and the bird is trapped.

There is little doubt that using any type of trap can prove a lengthy process, but if you are not adept at using a net, then it is the only method to employ. If the breeding season is already underway at the time when you wish to catch a bird (or birds), the only correct method is to use a baited trap, otherwise you could disturb the other breeding pairs so much that they will desert their nests.

When catching caged birds, it is important to carry out the procedure as quickly and as quietly as you possibly can. Try to approach the bird by directing your hand above and behind it, forcing the bird to fly up against the cage front. You should then be able to take hold of the bird easily by gently closing your hand around it.

If the cage is fairly large and contains a number of birds, and if the cage is the type which can be divided with a slide (see CAGES), then it is often possible to coax the actual bird you wish to catch into a section of the cage, slide the divider into place, and then catch the bird without causing distress to the other birds with which it is housed (see HANDLING).

CHARCOAL GRANULES
Gouldian Finches require a constant supply of charcoal granules to detoxify the stomach and intestines; hens, especially, will take large amounts when breeding. Many other species will also take these granules and they are best supplied by placing a small amount in a dish which is set on the floor of the cage or, in the case of aviary or flight birds, next to the food pots at the feeding station. Once a week, any granules remaining in the dish should be discarded and the dish thoroughly washed and replenished.

Iodized minerals resemble charcoal granules, except that they are of a finer texture, and these can usually be purchased, loose or packaged in polyethylene bags, from most shops which deal in pigeon requisites. Bicheno Finches are especially fond of these minerals. Unlike charcoal granules,

Charcoal granules for Gouldian and other Australian finches.

Gouldian Finches (4)

Black-headed Gouldian Finch (hen) – White-breasted mutation. Note the pure white chest-band and compare it with the beige-colored chest-band of the Lilac-breasted hen depicted below right.

Red-headed Gouldian Finch (cock) – Lilac-breasted mutation. This mutation first became available in 1978. The mutation has never become universally popular and, with more colorful mutations appearing, the Lilac-breasted could eventually disappear if concerted efforts are not made to keep it going.

The Lilac-breasted is recessive to the Normal but is dominant to the White-breasted. If a Lilac-breasted is mated to a White-breasted bird, a percentage of Lilac-breasteds will be produced. The mutation is available in all head colors.

Black-headed Gouldian Finch (hen) – Lilac-breasted mutation. Confusion often arises when one is attempting to distinguish between a Lilac-breasted hen and a White-breasted, and the parentage of the bird needs to be known before proper identification can be made. However, as can be seen, the Lilac-breasted hen has a somewhat beige-colored chest-band, whereas the White-breasted bird has a pure white chest-band.

Red-headed Gouldian Finch (cock) – Blue-backed mutation.

This mutation, as the name suggests, is blue wherever the Normal Gouldian is green. As the mutation lacks the ability to manufacture lutein, all the other colors are diluted, hence the Red- and Orange-headed appear as brownish-yellow, with the yellow of the abdomen paler than in the Normal.

Red-headed Gouldian Finch (cock) – Dilute-backed mutation.

This mutation does not manufacture melanin in the feathers of the back and wings and because of this they are yellow or pale greenish-yellow in color. The mutation also affects the color of the head (in a Black-headed bird) and tail (in all head colors), therefore these feathers are grayish. Other parts of the body are usually as intense in color as they are in the Normal Gouldian Finch.

however, I do not supply them ad lib, but place a small amount on the cage floor, next to the grit dish, about once a week. The birds usually eat these minerals immediately so there is little chance of them becoming soiled with droppings.

CHERRY FINCH (see PLUM-HEADED FINCH)

CHESTNUT-BREASTED FINCH (*Lonchura castaneothorax*)
The total length is approximately 101 mm (4 in). The crown, nape, and hindneck are grayish-brown, lightly flecked with brown. The mantle and wings are dark brown; the rump and upper-tail coverts are straw-yellow. The tail is yellowish; the lores, sides of the face, and the chin are black, as is the throat. The breast is chestnut, bordered along the lower edge and sides with black. The abdomen and under-tail coverts are white. The beak is bluish-gray. The sexes are similar (see MONOMORPHIC SPECIES).

The Chestnut-breasted Finch is found from the Kimberley region in northwestern Australia, across the Top End, irregularly in Cape York, and down the east coast, as far south as Nowra, New South Wales. Its preferred habitat is tall, rank grass and reeds along the edges of swamps, mangroves, and rivers. It can also be found in cultivated areas, such as cane fields, and among irrigated crops such as rice and millet.

Sometimes called the Chestnut-breasted Mannikin, this species is probably the most popular of the Australian mannikins, and is most certainly the one most commonly bred. It is often stated that the species is difficult to breed under caged conditions, but this is incorrect, as nowadays many youngsters are produced from pairs housed in cages.

The species is fairly hardy and will adapt well to life in an aviary (where it must have access to a heated shelter), an indoor flight, or a roomy box-type cage. The Chestnut-breasted will readily hybridize with other members of the mannikin family, therefore if it is to be housed in a mixed collection, such species as the Yellow-rumped Finch, the Society Finch, and Indian or African mannikins (munias) should be avoided.

Sexing the Chestnut-breasted can prove difficult, especially for someone new to the species. The cock usually has a silver-gray crown and nape, the hen being gray. Also, the breast of the cock is

Chestnut-breasted Finches at four days of age.

Chestnut-breasted
Finches at ten days
of age.

Chestnut-breasted
Finches at 18 days
of age.

usually a deeper chestnut than that of the hen, and the black band across the lower breast is wider in the cock. The ideal way in which to sex the species, however, is by the cock's song. Most cocks are extremely vocal and when young birds are molting into adult plumage they will sing continuously (see SEXING).

The average clutch is from four to six. Incubation is shared by the cock and the hen and both birds remain on the nest during the night. The chicks hatch after approximately 12 days and, if well fed, they should be ready to be fitted with a closed-band at seven to eight days of age. The parent birds cease to brood the chicks when they are approximately a week old, especially if the weather at the time is warm or if the breeding pair is housed in a warm birdroom. The chicks leave the nest when they are approximately three weeks of age. A few days before they reach this age, care should be taken not to disturb them in any way, otherwise they will almost certainly leave the nest prematurely. At first they are extremely timid, but they gain confidence with each day and by the time they are ready to be weaned (usually at five weeks of age), they should have lost any nervous tendencies.

Chestnut-breasteds will, without doubt, rear chicks successfully on a diet of seeds and green food. It is, however, beneficial to supply some form of live food and most pairs will accept large quantities of mealworms during the rearing period. Once the chicks are weaned, adults appear to lose all interest in live food until they have chicks again (see LIVE FOOD).

There are two established mutations in the Chestnut-breasted Finch: the Fawn and the Crested. It is almost certain that the latter has been obtained by mating a Crested Society Finch to a Chestnut-breasted and then mating any of the young which had crests back to pure Chestnut-breasted. By continually mating the crested birds back to pure Normals, eventually 'pure' Chestnut-breasteds carrying crests are produced.

I have read reports of an Albino mutation being bred in Australia, also of specimens which have a deep chocolate-brown chest band rather than the normal light brown. The latter is not an actual mutation, but has been produced by selective breeding.

CLAWS

The claws of most Australian finches require trimming at least twice a year. Australian mannikins (i.e., Chestnut-breasted, Pictorella, and Yellow-rumped Finches) may require their claws to be trimmed more frequently, especially if housed in cages.

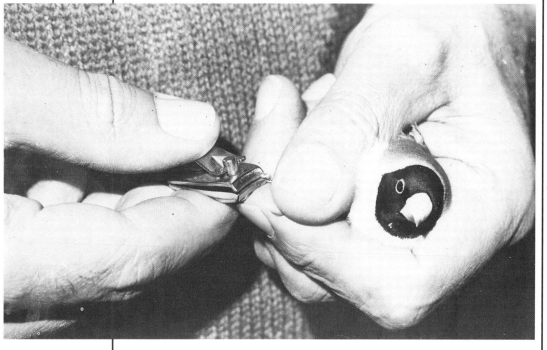

Trimming the claws of a Gouldian Finch. Note the correct way in which to hold a bird during this procedure.

The claws of all Australian finches are almost certain to require trimming before breeding commences and this can be carried out when the birds are caught prior to being placed in their breeding quarters. Occasionally breeding pairs may have to be caught for claw trimming before they have completed their breeding season. If this is the case, then the best time to do this is during the period between the first and second clutch, immediately after the first round of chicks has been weaned. The claws of breeding birds should be inspected again before they are placed in their resting quarters, otherwise the birds may have to be caught while molting. The stress this would create could seriously affect the birds, especially if they were in full molt.

To trim the claws, a bird should be caught and held firmly but gently in the hand with the foot held steady between finger and thumb, spreading the toes at the same time. To locate the vein, the foot should be held up to the light. With a sharp pair of scissors or nail clippers (the latter being by far the superior tool), a small portion of the claw should be trimmed off. Care must be taken not to cut the vein, otherwise severe bleeding may occur. Should one accidentally cut into the vein and cause bleeding, a moistened styptic pencil (as used for shaving cuts) should be applied to the end of the claw. If the bird is held in the hand for a few moments, the flow of blood should cease and the bird can then be released into its quarters.

CLOSED-BANDS (RINGS)
If a breeder wishes to keep records of all birds bred each season, then it is essential to fit chicks with closed-bands. Such bands are usually of anodized aluminum and are supplied in a different color for each year, thus enabling the year of a bird's birth to be seen at a glance. Each band is numbered, with the numbers usually running consecutively. The year of issue is also stamped on the band and, if required, the breeder's initials can also appear. The actual size of the band is also given, and if one is a member of a specialist society, the initials of the society may also appear on the band.

Fitting closed-bands to most Australian finch chicks is a simple procedure, especially if the parent birds are housed in cages. Obviously, it may prove more difficult to closed-band the chicks of birds breeding in aviaries. However, if the adult pairs can be persuaded to use nest boxes in the shelter, then no problems should arise. If a breeder finds it impractical to closed-band chicks, then I can only suggest that if strict records are to be kept on all birds bred, plastic split bands are used. (See SPLIT BANDS, RECORD-KEEPING.)

The majority of Australian finch

RECOMMENDED CLOSED-BAND SIZES

Beautiful Firetail	not known
Bicheno Finch	B *
Black-throated Finch	C
Blue-faced Parrot Finch	C
Chestnut-breasted Finch	C *
Crimson Finch	C
Diamond Firetail	D
Gouldian Finch	C
Long-tailed Grassfinch (and Heck's)	C
Masked Grassfinch	C
Painted Firetail	C
Pictorella Finch	C *
Plum-headed Finch	C
Red-browed Finch	C
Red-eared Firetail	not known
Star Finch	C
Yellow-rumped Finch	C *

*Manufacturers may recommend a different size but I have found this the most suitable in practice.

Below:
Closed-banding,
phase 1.

Bottom:
Closed-banding,
phase 2.

chicks are ready for closed-banding at ten days of age and it is desirable to check chicks of this age to see if closed-bands can be fitted. Should the chicks not be ready, then one would have to try again in a day or so.

Parent birds should never be forced from the nest, but both birds can usually be found away from the nest at some period in the day and the opportunity should then be taken to fit closed-bands. The chick should be taken up in the hand and placed in the crook of the fingers, with the head resting on one's forefinger. The leg and rear toe should be held between the thumb and the tip of the forefinger, with the front toes pointing straight ahead. To keep the toes together, draw them

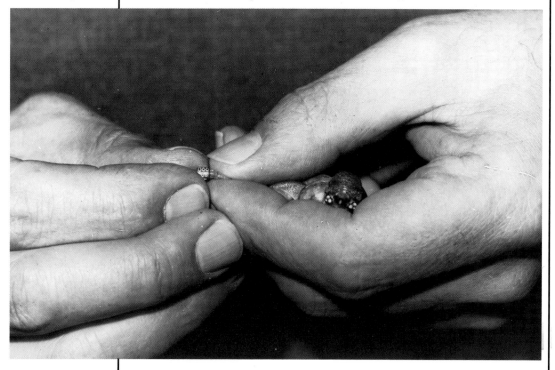

through the fingers which have first been liberally moistened with saliva, straightening the toes at the same time (**phase 1**). The band should then be slipped over the toes, eased over the joint and finally over the back toe (**phase 2**). If the band cannot be moved far enough up the leg to release the back toe, ease the toe out of the band with a sharpened matchstick or wooden toothpick (**phase 3**). Test to see if the band is easily slipped off the foot (**phase 4**); if it feels secure, then the chick can be placed back in the nest. If the closed-band slips over the foot too easily, then there is every possibility that the chick is too young and you will have to attempt to fit the band again in a day or so.

I find it preferable to remove all

Below: Closed-banding, phase 3.

Bottom: Closed-banding, phase 4.

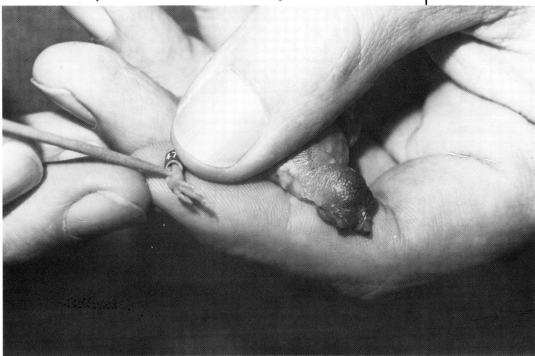

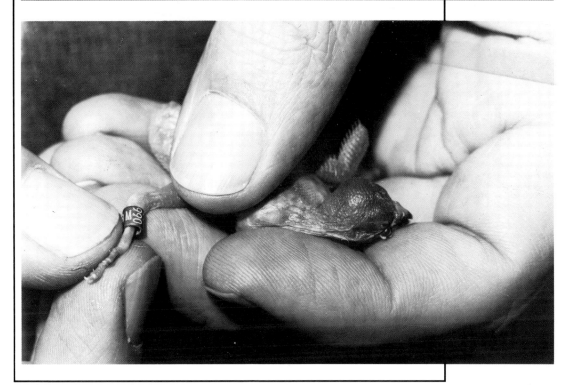

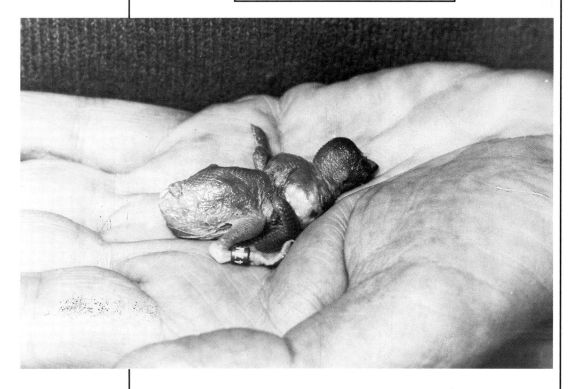

A Gouldian Finch chick immediately after being fitted with a closed-band.

chicks from the nest when closed-banding. Then, as each chick is successfully banded, it can immediately be returned to the nest. Not all the chicks from one nest necessarily hatch at the same time, as with certain species incubation commences before the final egg of the clutch is laid. If this is the case, then you may have to band the chicks over a period of days, rather than all at the same time.

A final point: Before closed-banding chicks, wash your hands and ensure that they are warm before taking up a chick. If you intend to fit bands to a number of chicks from different nests, wash your hands each time you have completed a nest.

COMPATIBILITY
The majority of Australian finches are highly sociable birds and have, in most cases, a docile nature. However, such species as the Crimson Finch, Beautiful Firetail, and Red-eared Firetail are exceptions to this generalization. The two Firetails are usually only aggressive toward others of their own kind. The Crimson Finch is not only aggressive toward its own kind but toward other species also. With the exception of these three species, most other Australian finches can be housed on the

colony system in an outdoor aviary or large indoor flight. Personally, I am not in favor of mixing species, but for those who wish to do so, careful consideration should be given to the requirements of each species you intend to keep.

For those of you who wish to linebreed your birds, or require young from a particular pair but prefer to house your birds in aviaries rather than cages, then if only one pair of each species you wish to keep is housed in an aviary or flight, control could be maintained over the individual pairs. However, before actually mixing species together, certain considerations must be taken into account. Closely related species should never be housed together, otherwise hybrids, rather than pure stock, may be produced. This means that such species as Long-tailed and Heck's Grassfinches should not be housed together or with similar species such as Black-throated (Parson) Finches and Masked Grassfinches. No more than one pair of Australian mannikins should be housed in an aviary, as Chestnut-breasted and Yellow-rumped Finches will readily hybridize, as may Pictorella Finches.

Certain species, such as Diamond Firetails, Black-throated (Parson) Finches, and Long-tailed (and Heck's) Grassfinches can prove somewhat overinquisitive concerning the nests of other birds with which they are housed. These species may also tend to be domineering. It is obvious, therefore, that careful consideration must be employed before different species are placed together, as it would be asking for trouble to place small species, such as Bicheno Finches, in with Long-tails or Diamond Firetails.

Stars, Plum-headed (Cherries), Bichenos, Gouldians, and Red-brows should live together peaceably. As long as the hybrid factor is taken into account, the more robust species, such as Diamond Firetails, Long-tails (and Heck's), Black-throated (Parson), Masked, Chestnut-breasteds, Yellow-rumped, Pictorellas, and Blue-faced Parrot Finches, should also live together fairly well. The main point to remember is that if you intend to house your birds in a mixed collection, then strict observation must be kept, at least until they have settled into their quarters. Obviously a small amount of bickering will be inevitable, but as long as serious fighting does not break out, the occasional flurry can be ignored.

For those who do not wish to linebreed their birds, or do not require young from any particular

pair of birds, then, of course, an aviary or flight can be given over to one particular species rather than a mixture. An aviary housing a small flock of one species can look most attractive. If it is a species that is highly social, then not only should breeding results prove satisfactory, but the owner will, no doubt, obtain much enjoyment from observing the birds going about their everyday lives in a natural way.

A variety of other small birds can be successfully housed with Australian finches. These include most foreign finches, quail, small pigeons or doves, softbills, and in certain cases even small parrotlike birds. With foreign finches, it should be remembered that Asiatic and/or African mannikins (munias) should not be housed with Australian mannikins, otherwise there is the possibility of hybrids being produced.

If you decide to keep a mixed collection, I would suggest that any youngsters be removed the moment they are seen to be independent. Certain species, such as Stars and Gouldians, if left to mature in a mixed aviary or flight, may attempt to imitate the songs of the other species with which they are housed. If they do, they may, when adult, refuse to mate with their own kind and thus fail to breed correctly.

Star Finches are compatible with Bicheno Finches and the two species are seen here housed in a community aviary.

A Star Finch × Bicheno Finch hybrid. This is a hybrid not previously recorded (see compatibility, page 38).

COURTSHIP DISPLAY

According to Immelmann (*Australian Finches,* 1985), the courtship behavior of Australian finches usually comprises three stages. First the cock and hen hop around each other, turning their heads and tails inwards. The cock then performs a dance and in certain other species a courtship song also.

The actual courtship dance may vary considerably between species, but usually consists of a series of vertical bobbing movements made on the spot by the male. Some species remain on the perch throughout the dance, but others may jump a fraction above it. In some species the cock (also the hen in the Star Finch) carries a long grass stem during the courtship ritual. Immelmann referred to this as a 'nesting symbol.' He noted that other species that did not carry any kind of nesting symbol made use instead of repetitive movements like 'beak-wiping, bowing and body-shaking.'

The final stage of the courtship behavior is when the hen solicits the cock to mate with her. She does this, according to Immelmann, by holding her tail either straight out or pointing upward, and then vibrating it. Most other passerine hens vibrate their wings.

Even under captive conditions, certain species of Australian finch will readily perform the courtship display. Obviously the display is more likely to be performed by birds housed in aviaries or large indoor flights; nevertheless, many species, even when housed in cages, will at least perform part of the courtship display.

Note on sources: (i) The courtship display of certain species has been observed only rarely and although I have observed courtship behavior in many of the better-known Australian finches, I have not witnessed the display of the rarer or little known species. To make this particular section as complete as possible, I have, therefore, in certain cases, used descriptions given by others. Where this is the case, I have named the author and given a reference to the original publication.

(ii) Acknowledgement is made to Klaus Immelmann, whose authoritative descriptions of the displays have been of very great value in compiling these notes. This applies to the Bicheno Finch, Gouldian Finch, Long-tailed/Heck's Grassfinch, Masked Grassfinch, Pictorella Finch and Plum-headed Finch.

Beautiful Firetail

The courtship display of this species has never been witnessed in the wild; indeed, as far as I am aware, it has only ever been observed by one person, namely Brian O'Gorman (Stawell, Victoria, Australia). As well as successfully breeding the Beautiful Firetail for four generations, O'Gorman has also written a detailed account of the courtship display in this species. It appeared, in *Australian Aviculture* 38, pp. 7–24, January 1984, under the title 'A field study of the Beautiful Firetail Finch.'

O'Gorman first observed a cock fly to a horizontal branch with a long piece of grass (approximately 200 mm/8 in) in its beak, held by the thicker end. The bird alighted on the branch and, still holding the grass, proceeded to nod its head three times. No sound was made, which led the author to believe that the grass-carrying display was a visual sign to the hen, who alighted some 150 mm (6 in) from the cock on the same branch. The cock then released the grass and, crouching low, inclined his body forward and downward until his head was well below the perch and the angle of his body, from beak to tail, was approximately 60 degrees. The tail was fanned and the wings were lowered and slightly opened, thus displaying the vivid red rump. The cock then inclined his head toward the hen and, while singing, with beak agape, bobbed his body up and down. The head bobs, the actual body movements, and the song phases (which are described as 'caw, caw, caw') all occurred in a series of three. While the cock sang, the hen hopped rapidly closer to him with her tail angled toward him (but not quivering her tail as do most other species). On the approach of the hen, the pair flew rapidly to ground cover and, because of this, copulation was not observed.

It appears that the actual bobbing motions of the cock in display are totally different to those of all other Australian finches. At the height of the bob, the bird appears to arch its body and the bobs seem to be carried out in slow motion. They are always conducted in a series of three, as are most phases of the whole courtship display.

Bicheno Finch

During the courtship display, the plumage of the cock is fully fluffed so that the body appears spherical. The cock crouches low over the perch, parallel to the hen, with his head turned toward her. In this position he may sing and/or bill-wipe. Should the hen move away, the cock will chase after her and again take up the position already described. A responsive hen will, in a matter of seconds after courtship has begun, crouch low on the perch and, with quivering tail, invite the cock to mount her. Copulation then takes place immediately.

Compared with many species of Australian finch, the courtship display of the cock Bicheno is fairly simple and is usually quickly over. Indeed, many cock birds, when presented with a hen in full breeding condition, rarely take up the courtship postures at all, but merely chase after her for a few seconds, after which copulation takes place without further preliminaries.

The Bicheno Finch is one of the species which will use a nesting symbol as part of the display. As with the other Australian finch species which use a symbol, the Bicheno prefers a somewhat thick piece of grass, usually some 200 mm (8 in) in length. Throughout the sequence, the cock faces his respective hen; he then gives a series of bows with his beak held in a horizontal position. As the cock becomes upright after each bow, his legs are stretched to their utmost and the feet, on occasions, appear to leave the perch (no more than 3 mm). At all times, the grass is held at the very end of its length and the sequence may be carried out for at least two or three minutes before the grass is eventually released. During the procedure described, the cock remains totally silent and the moment the nesting symbol is released the bird appears to lose all interest in the hen for a time.

Lone cocks will often perform the nest symbol display, and mated birds will often also carry out the display while the hen is incubating.

Black-throated (Parson) Finch

In this species (and also in the Long-tailed, Heck's, and Masked Grassfinch) head-bobbing is used habitually as an appeasing greeting between mates and flock members. Members of a pair, or a bird attempting to form a pair, usually combine it with turning the head and angled tail towards the partner.

During the actual courtship display, the body feathers of the cock are fluffed, those of the gray parts of the head rather more so, with the black feathers of the bib raised so that the lower part is brought forward, thus making the bib more conspicuous. With adult cocks a nesting symbol is rarely used (I have yet to witness an adult cock take up the symbol); however, young cock birds will regularly take up a nesting symbol when practising courtship rituals. The cock uses the bobbing ritual, during which either one or both feet leave the perch. The cock rarely sings during the bobbing movements, but the moment these cease he usually commences to sing while standing in an erect position with the head (and sometimes his body) facing the hen.

Hens solicit with quivering tail, and after copulation has taken place the cock usually stands beside the hen for a moment or so, sometimes inviting allo-preening.

Blue-faced Parrot Finch

It is reported that during courtship display the cock Blue-faced Parrot Finch will hold pieces of nesting material in his bill (I have never witnessed this occurrence). Young birds appear to go through a more elaborate courtship display than more mature pairs. Indeed, the majority of mature cocks only carry out pursuit flights, when they chase after their respective hen until she eventually submits. Copulation then takes place.

During mating, the cock takes hold of the hen's head or nape feathers, in certain cases actually plucking feathers out. This is one of the reasons why many Blue-faced hens (especially when caged) lose their head feathers.

Chestnut-breasted Finch

Chestnut-breasted cocks are extremely vocal and can be heard singing for hours at a time. Some will even sing while incubating. The courtship display consists of the cock raising the back and rump feathers, with the feathers of the lower breast and belly also puffed out. The cock stands sideways on the perch, facing the hen, and performs bobbing movements, singing the whole time. At no time do his feet leave the perch. After a few moments the hen will crouch and solicit by quivering her tail. The cock then mounts her.

In *Australian Finches* (1985), Immelmann has described what he refers to as 'the second part of the courtship.' During this procedure the pair remain very close and make several low bows in unison with one another. Each bird positions its tail toward its partner and fluffs out its body feathers to the fullest possible extent. At such times, both birds will also open their beaks wide, although, unlike the display phase described earlier, the cock bird does not sing during this latter performance.

I am greatly indebted to the work of Klaus Immelmann for this information, as I have yet to witness the second part of the courtship display for myself. However, I would add that bachelor cocks that are housed together will often perform a similar display.

Crimson Finch

The cock Crimson Finch, holding a piece of grass in his beak, flies toward, and usually lands a short distance from, the hen. He then hops toward her and, with the feathers of his face, back and underparts fluffed out, in a near horizontal posture with angled tail and head turned toward the hen, the cock bobs up and down, bowing low as he does so. Immediately prior to copulation taking place, the cock assumes an erect posture, still continuing to bob up and down. If the hen then solicits with quivering tail, copulation will take place immediately.

The full courtship display is rarely observed in captive birds. Also, a captive cock bird appears to show more aggression toward the hen than wild birds do. This is due, no doubt, to the birds being in a somewhat confined area. When caged, the cock bird may perform little or no courtship behavior, but continually chase after the hen until she submits, when copulation then takes place.

Diamond Firetail

In the wild, this species performs a most elaborate courtship display, usually on a high dead branch. Under captive conditions only a small part of the display may be used, even when birds are housed in fairly large aviaries.

The use of a nesting symbol is most pronounced in this species and the cock bird usually selects the longest, stiffest piece of grass he can find. Before beginning the actual display, the cock bird usually arranges his feathers with shaking movements, so that the spotted flank feathers are outside of the folded wings and therefore fully displayed. With the grass firmly held in his beak, the cock stretches his neck upward, but with his head turned downward so that the beak is almost touching, and nearly parallel to, the neck. The feathers of the neck are sleeked, with the remainder of the body feathers, especially those of the belly, fluffed out. In this position, the cock bobs up and down, stretching and flexing the legs, but not letting go of the perch. He will then sing and, as the hen comes closer, he at first intensifies his display then bows low toward, and in front of her, opening his beak and turning his head up toward her, thus simulating the begging posture of fledglings.

In this species copulation takes place in the nest, although an extremely virile cock may attempt to mate with the hen without first entering the nest.

Gouldian Finch

Courtship behavior in this species is highly ritualized and the feather postures of the cock are

Normal Diamond Firetail.

Long-tailed Grassfinch.

specialized, thus presenting the colorful plumage markings to the greatest advantage. The feathers of the forehead are slightly erected and those of the occiput fully erected, thus enlarging the bright head colors and framing them with the turquoise-blue band and the grass-green back. The feathers of the breast and belly are fluffed out, so that the vivid chest band is enlarged, and the lifting of the tail ensures that the turquoise-blue rump feathers are more conspicuous.

Courtship commences with the cock perched in front of, or beside the hen, in an almost horizontal position with his tail lifted at an angle of some 45 degrees. He then begins a series of ritualised double bill-wipes. The bill-wiping then becomes more rapid until it is no longer possible to see the individual movements of the head, and by now the beak no longer touches the perch. The cock will then go into an upright posture, with the whole of the body drawn rigidly back and the tail held at an angle and slightly depressed. The cock then begins to sing, with the beak pointing downward and the head moving from side to side. While singing, he will bob up and down rapidly, alternately stretching and flexing his legs, with or without the feet leaving the perch. There is, apparently, considerable variation in the performance of different cock birds. Some of the actions described above may be emphasised, minimised or omitted altogether.

Copulation usually occurs in the nest, to which the cock, followed by the hen, often flies immediately after the courtship display. However, in captive birds mating may, on rare occasions, take place on the perch.

Long-tailed Grassfinch (also Heck's)

The courtship display of this species is very similar to that described for the Black-throated Finch. As with the latter, it appears that only young males use a piece of coarse grass as a nesting symbol,

Fawn Heck's Grassfinch.

and even then only a small proportion of young male birds of this species seem to carry out this procedure.

In *Australian Finches* (1985), Immelmann has recorded that immediately after copulation has taken place, the cock comes to perch beside the hen, where he performs a deep bow, turning his head to one side so that his black throat patch is clearly visible. The Long-tailed and the Black-throated are the only grassfinches which have ever been seen to carry out these distinctive post-copulatory displays.

Masked Grassfinch

The courtship display of the Masked is similar to that of the Black-throated and Long-tailed Grassfinch. However, no nesting symbol is used, even by young males.

Immelmann states that the Masked Grassfinch may repeat both the courtship display and copulation several times and that copulation itself may last for as long a period as 20 seconds.

Painted Firetail

In the *Avicultural Magazine* 52: 149–158 (1946), L.C. Webber described the courtship display of the Painted thus: 'The male held a grass-stalk in his bill, crouched over the perch, bobbed up and down and more or less performed the Diamond Sparrow [*sic*] display.' I have not yet seen this display for myself.

Since the above description appeared, other authors have also given a similar description of the Painted Firetail display and no doubt this will soon be well documented.

In the wild, the courtship ritual usually takes place on the ground, however captive birds usually, if not always, perform from a perch. This display is usually prefaced by a greeting display or by both cock and hen repeatedly picking up and dropping twigs, small stones, or other such objects that are to be found on the ground.

When ready to mate, the hen angles her tail toward the cock and then, with quivering tail, solicits in the usual manner, after which mating takes place almost immediately.

Pictorella Finch

This species always courts on the ground (or if caged on the floor of the cage). The courtship usually commences with both the cock and the hen making pecking movements directed at the ground. If available to them, they may pick up small stones, sticks, or such and quickly drop them again.

The actual courtship display has two phases, with the cock first taking up a piece of grass in his beak. Then, according to Immelmann, he points his beak upward, fluffs out his feathers and spreads his tail. Maintaining this appearance, he hops back and forth in an arc before the hen. His movements become quicker and quicker and he hops closer and closer until he is directly in front of her. It should be mentioned that although I have described the cock as taking up a nesting symbol, many cocks regularly display without a symbol.

At the commencement of part two of the display, the cock (if he has, in fact, used a nesting symbol) releases the piece of grass and quickly hops to the rear of the hen until his body is parallel to hers. In this position, with tail fanned out and slightly turned toward the hen, the cock makes a deep bow. This procedure may be repeated several times until the hen begins to quiver her tail (thus inviting copulation).

Plum-headed Finch (Cherry Finch)

There is much variation in the courtship display of this species. Certain cocks will use a grass stem as a nesting symbol, others never do so. Indeed, none of the cock birds I have owned have ever been observed using a nesting symbol during the display.

According to Immelmann, if the symbol is used it will take the form of a grass stem held in the tip of the cock's beak. Singing continuously, he settles close to the hen and begins to bob slowly up and down without letting go of his perch, all the while holding his beak straight out or even angled toward the ground. He turns his tail only a fraction in the direction of the hen. The body is held upright with throat and belly feathers slightly puffed out. The red throat feathers are puffed out slightly, as are the white ear coverts. After several bobbing movements, the cock releases the piece of grass and repeats his song (sometimes with his beak wide open). Beak-wiping is frequently practiced. Shortly afterward, if the hen is receptive, copulation takes place.

Red-browed Finch

Desmond Morris (in *Proceedings of the Zoological Society of London*, 131, 389–439, 1958), described the courtship display of this species as follows:

> The male selects a long piece of straw, holds it in his beak, advances to the side of the other bird and begins to sing and dance with vertical movements. These are only slightly directed towards the other, the male being almost broadside-on. The body is now extremely erect, with the legs stretched and the head held back, the beak pointing to the sky. The vertical inverted-curtsy jumps are so vigorous that, as in the Gouldian Finch, the male's feet leave the perch each time. The tail is held more downwards now and is strongly twisted towards the female. This display

attracts her and she approaches the male. As she alights near him, she throws back her head and, for a few moments, holds this position with her beak pointing upwards like his.

Shortly before mating takes place, the cock usually releases the piece of grass. However, certain authors have observed the nesting symbol still being held by the cock even when copulation is taking place.

Red-eared Firetail

In the wild the courtship display of this species usually takes place high up in trees and, because of this, little has been written about the actual display.

Few aviculturists have seen the display, however it has been described by Landolt, Burkard, and Ziswiler (in *Bonner Zoologische Beitraege 26*, 1975). These authors describe the cock bird as holding a piece of grass in his beak and arching his body until his head is below the perch. The hen sometimes assumes the same position. Her tail is kept erect and slightly bent toward her partner. Likewise, her head is turned toward her partner. During the first

Pictorella Finch (hen).

Painted Firetail (cock).

phase of the courtship song, the cock, in the arched position, approaches the hen. As he comes close to her he continues to sing but straightens up at the end of each song phase and bobs up and down by alternately bending and stretching his legs, without actually leaving the perch. As soon as the hen is ready to mate, she starts to quiver her tail in a somewhat horizontal position. The cock then releases the grass and copulation takes place.

Star Finch

In this species, the hen has a display flight in which she flies around a perched cock in a fluttering butterfly-like flight while holding a long piece of grass in the tip of her beak. This display flight is performed especially by unattached hens and may perhaps stimulate cocks to courtship and pair-formation.

Immature (and adult) cocks, even when housed alone, will also carry out a similar display.

In the actual courtship display, the cock will hold a piece of grass in his beak (in captivity cocks will, if grass is unavailable, take up such things as strips of newspaper or feathers) and will then approach the hen with tail angled and the spotted feathers of the lores, breasts, and flanks erected. He bobs up and down, turning his body from side to side as he does so, his feet usually leaving the perch with each upward movement, after which he makes a deep bow. When jumping, each time the cock lands on the perch he is a little nearer to the hen. His beak is usually held in a horizontal position, but at a later stage in the display, just prior to attempts at copulation, the beak, with an upward movement, is jerked to an angle of 45 degrees. The song is heard frequently during display.

If the hen solicits with quivering tail, the cock will immediately mount her and copulation will take place. It is reported that during copulation the cock will often hold on to the nesting symbol. I have never actually witnessed this, as all the cocks I have observed have always released the grass stalk prior to mating.

Yellow-rumped Finch

The courtship display of the Yellow-rumped Finch is similar to that of the Chestnut-breasted, except that it is more exaggerated, with more beak-wiping and fluffing of the feathers.

CRIMSON FINCH (*Neochmia phaeton*) (color photos on page 114)
The approximate overall size is 130 mm (5 in). The adult cock, from forehead to rump and wings, is earth-brown with a blackish gloss on the head and a crimson wash on the mantle and wings (more noticeable on the latter). The upper-tail coverts are bright crimson; the tail is dull crimson; the lores, superciliary, sides of the face, chin to breast and flanks are bright crimson, spotted with pure white on the latter. The center of the abdomen and the under-tail coverts are black. The beak is red. The hen is paler on the upperparts than the cock and the crimson is restricted to her face and throat, with the remainder of the underparts ashy, with white spotting along the flanks. (See DIMORPHIC SPECIES.)

The subspecies *evangelinae* (see later) is sufficiently distinct to be given its own common name of Pale or White-bellied Crimson Finch. Where *phaeton* has the abdomen and under-tail coverts black, *evangelinae* is white. It also has the base of the beak gray.

Distribution is from southern New Guinea across northern Australia from the Kimberley region in Western Australia through the top of the Northern Territory to isolated pockets of northern Cape York Peninsula, and from the Atherton region south to Mackay. The habitat is mainly wet grassland areas near creeks and streams, bordered by eucalypt woodland and pandanus palms. The species appears to have a particular association with this palm, as it nests in it and feeds on

Crimson Finch (cock)

the seeds. The Crimson may also be found near farmland, in gardens and parks and has even been recorded as nesting in human dwelling houses.

As already mentioned, there are two subspecies, namely the Black-bellied (*N. p. phaeton*) and the White-bellied (*N. p. evangelinae*). The former occupies the bulk of the species' range, from the Northern Territory to the Kimberley region and from the Atherton region to Mackay. The White-bellied race is found in the Cape York region and southern New Guinea.

Both forms are rare in captivity and because of this the species is one of the most expensive of all the Australian finches to purchase. Crimson Finches have a reputation for being aggressive, not only to their own kind, but to other birds with which they may be housed. However, it is now thought that much of the supposed aggression is, in fact, part of the mating display and is therefore harmless. Nevertheless, if you intend to house a pair with other species in a flight, strict observation should be maintained, especially during the breeding season, as the many reports of other species being attacked, and in some cases killed by Crimsons, cannot all be hearsay.

The ideal way to house a breeding pair of Crimson Finches is to give a small aviary over to them alone. They are not particularly hardy and a heated shelter, to which they could retire should the need arise, would be a must. Housed in such a way, a compatible pair should breed successfully. If the pair can be persuaded to take to a nest box in the aviary shelter, rather than build their own nest in the planted flight, then so much the better. No doubt aviculturists who reside in countries where cold, damp winters are the norm would prefer to house such a rare and expensive species in a roomy cage in a birdroom. The main criterion is to ensure you have a compatible pair. Therefore, if two or more birds are purchased, it is a good idea to house a cock and hen in adjoining cages separated with a wire divider. Once the birds appear to have taken to each other, they could then, under supervision, be allowed together.

The average clutch ranges from four to eight eggs. Both birds take turns incubating, but it is usually the hen who sits during the night. Incubation does not usually commence in earnest until the majority of the clutch is laid. Brooding during the day may cease (especially during hot weather) when the chicks are between five to seven days old; the hen will, however, still brood the chicks during the night until they are at least nine days of age, after which both birds stay away from the nest during the night. The young usually leave the nest at three weeks, some if not all of the brood returning to the nest to sleep for a number of days after fledging.

The Crimson Finch has been bred successfully without the aid of live food. Nevertheless, if breeding pairs will accept live food it obviously gives the chicks a good start in life. Pairs with young should therefore be offered live ants' eggs, 'white' mealworms, and, if easily obtainable, small spiders and such. Soft food should also be supplied, as should large quantities of soaked seeds. (See LIVE FOOD, SOFT FOOD, SOAKED SEEDS.)

If a breeding pair is housed in a small aviary, then it is possible to leave the young with their parents. However, cage-bred young would have to be removed from their parents' cage the moment they were seen to be independent, otherwise they would almost certainly be attacked by the adults and might even be killed if left too long.

No mutations of the Crimson Finch have so far been established, although a 'yellow' phase has been produced, and a 'white' hen has also been reported as having been seen in the wild in 1985.

CUTTLEFISH BONE

Cuttlefish bone is the calcareous internal shell of the cuttlefish of the genus *Sepia*, quantities of which get washed up on beaches. It is not, of course, real bone, but is rich in lime, salt, and calcium. The shells or 'bones' are usually sold whole. They vary in length from about 15 to 25 cm (6–10 in), are oval in shape, and chalky-white in color. Being rich in calcium, cuttlefish bone aids the formation of eggshell and is also beneficial to the correct development of young, growing birds.

Firetails (1)

Diamond Firetail – Fawn mutation. This attractive mutation is well established and appears to be as robust as the Normal.

Diamond Firetail – Yellow mutation. As can be seen, the only color affected by this mutation is red, and because of this the rump and the beak are orange. The remainder of the plumage is as in the Normal.

Diamond Firetail –
Yellow/Fawn
mutation.
Here the Fawn
and the Yellow
mutations are
combined, thus
producing a bird
which is not only
fawn but also has
the orange rump
and beak of the
Yellow mutation.

Diamond Firetail,
often given the
misnomer
Diamond Sparrow.
  This is one of the
larger Australian
finches. Sexing can
prove extremely
difficult and the
only reliable
method is by the
song of the cock,
which consists of
very low raspy
calls.

Because of its nutritional importance, all Australian finches should be offered a constant supply of cuttlefish bone. For caged birds, a piece can be secured in a clip attached to the cage front. For aviary birds, the 'bone' should be secured next to a perch in the shelter.

The cuttlefish bone supplied must be dry and clean. Caged birds may, from time to time, soil their supply with droppings. Any which becomes soiled should be removed the moment it is seen and the soiled area cut away with a sharp knife. Flaked cuttlefish bone should also be supplied, especially during the breeding season. To flake the 'bone,' place it on a chopping board and, with a sharp knife, remove slivers of 'bone' until all that is left is the hard 'shell;' this should be discarded. I flake enough 'bone' to last about a week and this is stored in the birdroom in a closed dish so that it is always at hand.

Nonbreeding birds (such as resting adults and youngsters) can be offered small amounts about twice a week. I place the flaked 'bone' on top of the grit. Most Australian finches will immediately fly down to flaked cuttlefish bone and if only sufficient is offered for the birds to eat within half an hour or so, there should be little possibility of it becoming soiled before the birds have had a chance to consume it.

Hens, when laying, and pairs with chicks will often eat large amounts of flaked cuttlefish bone and a small amount can be offered each day if the birds are keen to take it.

DIAMOND FIRETAIL (*Emblema guttata*) (color photos on pages 50–51)
One of the larger Australian finches, the Diamond Firetail has an overall length of approximately 115–120 mm (4½–4¾ in). The head and nape are gray with whitish cheeks and a white throat. The lores are black; the mantle and wings are brown. The rump and upper-tail coverts are crimson; the tail is black. The center of the breast is black, the sides of the breast and the flanks are also black, each feather having a large subterminal white spot. The abdomen and under-tail coverts are white and the beak is red. The sexes are similar (see MONOMORPHIC SPECIES).

The range of the species extends from the southern Eyre Peninsula and Kangaroo Island in South Australia through most of Victoria and eastern New South Wales, on the island side of the Great Dividing Range, north to Carnarvon in Queensland. It inhabits eucalypt forest and open eucalypt woodland. It appears that its numbers have been declining considerably since the 1960s.

The Diamond Firetail (often called the Diamond Sparrow, especially in the USA and the UK) may be housed as a single pair in a small aviary or indoor flight, or in a large cage. However, for the best breeding results the species should be housed on the colony system (see later) in a fairly large planted aviary. Although one of the more robust of the Australian finches, the Diamond Firetail should not be subjected to low temperatures, especially when breeding, otherwise fertility may be severely reduced.

Sexing can prove extremely difficult, especially for a person with little or no experience of the species. Cock birds often have a more silvery-gray head than the hens; when in breeding condition the cocks have a maroon-colored beak, that of the hen being coral-pink. A more reliable method

Diamond Firetail—Fawn mutation.

of sexing is by the song of the cock bird, which consists of very low, raspy calls.

Diamond Firetail cocks have a most elaborate courtship display, which entails the bird taking up in its beak a selected piece of grass, usually the longest available. The bird then carries out elaborate movements, usually referred to as a 'dance' (see COURTSHIP DISPLAYS).

One of the reasons why colony breeding is preferable to housing a single pair on its own is that the species is somewhat sensitive as far as the selection of a mate is concerned. A cock and hen do not necessarily make a breeding pair, and a pair that are forced upon each other may not make any attempt to breed. Obviously this can become a problem if the bird keeper wishes to breed from a particular pair or a certain mutation. If you especially want a certain pair of birds to mate together, then they could at least be tried together in a cage or small flight. If they take to each other, then all is well and they can then

be released into the colony, as the majority of Diamond Firetails, once paired, remain so for life.

It is often stated that the Diamond Firetail, although an attentive parent, is generally intolerant of nest inspection, abandoning eggs or young at the least interference. This may be so when aviary birds are allowed to build their own nests among the shrubs or bushes in the flight area, as no doubt their owner would often find it difficult to inspect such a nest without causing a disturbance. However, large numbers of Diamonds are bred and closed-banded each year, so obviously the species is more tolerant of nest inspection than is sometimes made out. If a breeder wishes to closed-band all the youngsters he or she breeds, then it is preferable for Australian finches of all species to be persuaded to nest in the boxes provided, rather than allowed to build nests wherever they please. Caged birds have no option but to build in the nest box, but it could prove

Firetails (2)

Painted Firetail (cock). Often given the name Painted Finch, the Painted Firetail is extremely rare outside of Australian aviculture.

Painted Firetail pair. The cock is on the left.

This is one of the most beautiful of all the Australian finches. Being dimorphic, the sexes are easily identified. The cock bird has the face and upper throat vivid scarlet, with a large patch of scarlet on the center of the abdomen. Hens have only the lores, the feathers above the eyes and the base of the lower mandible scarlet. They are also more heavily spotted with white which extends under the chin.

Painted Firetails searching for fallen grass seeds.

The species spends a considerable amount of its time on the ground and in the wild feeds mostly on bare ground between tussocks of grass, picking up small grass seeds. This behavior is simulated in captive birds, and pairs housed in roomy cages will not only spend lengthy periods on the cage floor, but will also sleep there. Because of this, birds housed in cages should have their quarters cleaned at regular intervals, otherwise foot infections may occur.

Diamond Firetail chicks — Fawn mutation. The chicks are two to three days of age, with two eggs still to hatch. Note the clearly visible mouth markings in the chick with an open gape.

difficult to dissuade a persistent pair of aviary birds from building a nest in a planted flight, no matter how attractive you make the nest boxes appear.

The clutch usually consists of from five to six eggs (up to nine have been recorded). Incubation normally commences after the second egg has been laid. Both sexes share in incubation and care of the young, and during the night both birds will retire to the nest. Brooding usually ceases after ten days and the young leave the nest when they are between 24 to 26 days of age. Immature birds are similar in appearance to an adult except that the head is olive-gray, the flanks brown and the underparts white. The beak is grayish-black (see IMMATURE PLUMAGE).

At present there are only three

Diamond Firetail chicks.

mutations, namely the Yellow, in which the red of the rump is replaced with orange (the beak of this mutation may be a less intense red than that of a normal bird), the Fawn, and the Yellow/Fawn.

DIAMOND SPARROW (see DIAMOND FIRETAIL)

DIET (basic)

The basic diet for Australian finches should consist of good quality panicum millet, white millet, and plain canary seed. Many aviculturists offer a mixture of these seeds, usually referred to as 'foreign-finch mixture'. I prefer to offer seeds individually rather than as a mixture, as many species prefer one type of seed to another,

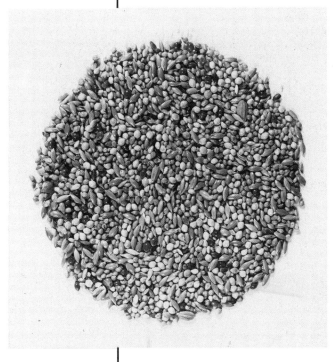

Foreign finch mixture. Although favored by some keepers, this can prove wasteful for birds that are choosy.

and if a mixture is given much can be wasted when the birds throw out seeds they are not partial to. Seeds should be offered either in earthenware bowls placed on the cage floor, or in a seedhopper attached to the wall of an aviary shelter or inside flight. Perches should be kept well away from the seeds, otherwise the latter could become fouled by droppings. (See CHARCOAL GRANULES, CUTTLEFISH BONE, EGGSHELL, GREEN FOOD, GRIT, LIVE FOOD, SEEDING GRASSES, SOAKED SEEDS, SOFT FOOD, SPRAY MILLET, WATER.)

DIGGLES FINCH (*Poephila cincta atropygialis*)

The Diggles Finch is a subspecies of the Black-throated (or Parson) Finch (see BLACK-THROATED FINCH) and differs from it only in that it has a black rump. In the United Kingdom it is usually known as the 'Black-rumped Parson Finch'; only in Australia is it referred to as Diggles. It is fairly widely kept in its country of origin but is extremely rare elsewhere. Unless a serious attempt is made to breed from these the subspecies could eventually be lost to aviculture outside of Australia.

As with the Black-rumped phase in the Bicheno Finch, the Black-rumped Diggles is recessive to the White-rumped. Any person in possession of a Black-rumped should mate it to a good-quality White-rumped; the resulting young would be visual White-rumps split for Black-rumped. These, in turn, could be mated to either Black-rumped or split birds. (See BICHENO FINCH for further details on color inheritance; also GENETICS.)

The Diggles is found in southern Cape York, west of the Leichardt river, north from Normanton to the Archer and Watson rivers.

As with the Black-throated Finch, there is also a Chocolate phase in the Diggles (*P. c. nigrotecta*) which has the rump black and the lower breast and abdomen grayish chocolate-brown. It is found in northern Cape York, north of the Archer and Watson rivers. Although secure in the wild, this form is rare in captivity, even in Australia. If the Chocolate phase (with the white rump) was mated to a Chocolate Diggles (which has a black rump), then I do not see why, eventually, the numbers of the latter should not be increased.

An Albino Diggles Finch has recently been reported as being bred in Australia. However, due no doubt to its great rarity, no mutations have so far appeared in stock held outside of Australia.

DIMORPHIC SPECIES (see page 60)

Star Finches (1)

Star Finch (hen). Adult Star Finches are easily sexed as hens have less red around the face and none on the chin. Hens also have more extensive white spotting across the throat and their overall body color is paler than in the cocks.

Immature Star Finch molting into sub-adult plumage.
Unlike other Australian finch species, the Star Finch has a sub-adult plumage phase. Young birds begin to molt from immature to sub-adult plumage when they are approximately eight weeks of age. When this molt is completed, the birds look very much like poorly colored adults. It may be seven to eight months before the birds again begin to molt. When this molt is completed, the birds will then be in full adult plumage.

Star Finch (cock). In the wild, there are two subspecies, namely *Neochmia ruficauda ruficauda* and *N. r. clarescens*. However, outside of Australian aviculture, the two races have become so interbred that it is now impossible to detect the slight differences in captive-bred birds.

Being fairly easy to breed, the Star Finch is an ideal species for the newcomer to Australian finches.

DIMORPHIC SPECIES, A GUIDE TO VISUAL SEXING

Species	Distinguishing features between adult birds cock (♂) and hen (♀)
Crimson Finch	Body color, ♂ bright crimson, ♀ dull olive-brown. Crown and nape, ♂ gray, ♀ olive-brown. Abdomen and under-tail coverts, ♂ black, ♀ pale creamy-fawn (except for white-bellied race).
Gouldian Finch	Breast, ♂ purple, ♀ paler. Beak color (when in breeding condition), ♂ white with colored tip, ♀ blackish. In general, the overall body color of ♀ is paler than that of the ♂.
Painted Firetail	Face and upper throat, ♂ vivid scarlet, ♀ only lores, feathers above eyes, and base of lower mandible scarlet. Center of abdomen, ♂ large scarlet patch, ♀ more heavily spotted with white and extending to under chin.
Pictorella Finch	Face and throat, ♂ glossy black edged with pale buff around ear coverts, ♀ brownish black. Breast, ♂ large white spots, almost continuous, flecked with black, ♀ smaller white spots, more heavily flecked with black.
Plum-headed Finch	Forehead, crown and chin, ♂ dark claret, ♀ less claret on forehead, none on crown and chin, also white eye-stripe above and extending past eye (absent in ♂). A well-colored ♂ also has more pronounced bars on the upper breast and flanks than ♀.
Star Finch	Facial area and chin, ♂ red, ♀ less red on facial area and none on chin, ♀ more extensive spotting across throat and overall body color paler.

DOMESTICATION

The term domestication is used to describe the process by which strains of wild animals are selectively and intensively bred by man. There are many avian examples, chiefly in the sphere of food production, notably among poultry, but also an increasing number in aviculture. For example, species such as the Canary, Budgerigar, Zebra Finch, and Society Finch are considered to be fully domesticated.

Nowadays many Australian finch species are bred in such large numbers, and are found in so many mutations, that I am surprised that at least some of them have not been declared fully domesticated. However, for this to come about requires a leading body to declare a species to be domesticated and to advertise the fact in journals and magazines relating to aviculture.

Species (or subspecies) which I consider should be declared domesticated include the Gouldian Finch, Star Finch, Heck's Grassfinch, Black-throated Finch, Blue-faced Parrot Finch, and Diamond Firetail.

In January, 1960, the Australian Government placed a ban on the exportation of any of its fauna. This means that all the Australian finches now held in captivity outside of Australia have derived from those already held at the time when the ban was imposed.

The extent to which certain Australian finch species have changed during the relatively short period since the ban was imposed is remarkable. Gouldian Finches, for instance, can now be persuaded to

Red-headed
Gouldian Finch
(cock).

breed successfully at any time of the year, whereas when mainly wild-caught birds were being kept, the majority would breed only during the months of December to April.

Certain species appear to be increasing in size. This is no doubt due to selective breeding, as, when a breeder selects his or her breeding stock each year, there is a tendency for the larger birds to be retained. Also, from my experience, when a breeder offers his or her surplus stock for sale, it is always the larger specimens which are sold first; even when the purchaser may be relatively new to Australian finches, he or she still usually selects the larger birds.

A further change which has come about is the number of mutations which have appeared in Australian finch species. In 1965 only one mutation (other than the two already occurring in the wild) was known in the Gouldian Finch, namely the White-breasted. Now so many mutations are available in this species alone that it is difficult to keep up with them all. Color mutations are well established in many other Australian finch species as well as the Gouldian (see the headings for individual species). There is even one feather

mutation, namely the crested form of the Chestnut-breasted Finch.

Whether or not the continual appearance and eventual establishment of all these mutations is desirable is debatable. Many aviculturists are voicing their doubts regarding this, as they feel that the 'pure' wild-type bird could eventually disappear from the avicultural scene. However, man has always been interested in creating something 'different' and bird breeders are no exception; as long as color (and feather) mutations continue to appear, there will always be those who are keen to breed and to attempt to establish them.

DOUBLE-BAR FINCH (see BICHENO FINCH)

Star Finches (2)

Star Finch (hen) – Pied mutation.
    The bird depicted appears to have only a very small area of pied plumage. As the red does not mask out the pied areas in the hen as it does in the cock (see below), many Pied Star Finch hens are heavily pied around the head.

Star Finch (cock) – Pied mutation. It is unfortunate that, at present, this mutation only appears to affect the extremities in the Star Finch, i.e. only feathers on the head, wings and tail may be pied, with the actual body feathers remaining normal. Another problem is that young cock birds, which may be heavily pied around the head while in immature plumage, lose this pied feathering once fully adult, due to the red masking out the pied areas.

Star Finch (hen) – Yellow mutation. This mutation is well established and well-colored birds are most attractive.

Star Finch (cock) – Yellow mutation.

This mutation affects the red areas, causing them to be bright orange-yellow. The white spotting also appears to be affected slightly, as all the Yellow Stars I have bred (and seen) appear to have larger spots than in the Normal, especially on the breast and flanks.

The mutation is firmly established and is bred in fairly substantial numbers annually.

E

EGG-BINDING

Egg-binding is a condition which may cause the death of valuable breeding hens if it is not noticed in time and dealt with immediately. The causes of this problem are many. Hens that are placed in their breeding quarters before they are in breeding condition are prone to the complaint, as are birds that are overweight, or birds that have not received a sufficiently nutritious diet before being allowed to breed. Old hens and those too young for breeding may also suffer from egg-binding.

Whatever the cause, a hen that is considered to be suffering from egg-binding should be caught immediately for inspection. One should feel very gently around the area of the vent. If an egg can be felt, then the hen is almost certainly egg-bound and should immediately be placed in a hospital cage, the temperature of which should be maintained at a constant 30°C (86°F). Food and water should be supplied; often a spray of millet will tempt the bird to feed. A few drops of lubricating jelly (K-Y®) or mineral oil placed carefully into the vent, may help to release the egg. Calcium injections stimulate normal contractions of the oviduct.

Some hens are reluctant to pass an egg while in the hospital cage. Therefore, if a bird has not passed an egg after being in the cage for a few hours, it may help to let the temperature fall to that of the birdroom (by turning off the controls of the hospital cage) and then return the bird to its breeding quarters. Very often the bird will enter the nest box and lay the egg without further trouble. Should this be the case, careful observation would have to be maintained to ensure that the bird lays the remainder of the clutch.

If the bird shows further symptoms of egg-binding, then she will again have to be placed in the hospital cage. This procedure may have to be repeated for each egg laid. Should such a bird complete the clutch and then begin to incubate, she should be treated normally as, in all probability, the eggs will hatch and the chicks will be reared successfully. Usually such a bird has no further problems after the rest from egg laying incurred by incubating and rearing chicks.

If a hen lays a *perfect* egg while in the hospital cage, the egg should be taken from the cage and placed in the nest box. The temperature of the hospital cage should be lowered to that of the birdroom or aviary and the hen returned to her quarters. If the breeding pair accept the egg (or eggs), there is every possibility that they will carry on breeding operations.

If a hen has difficulties in laying an egg, it is advantageous if the pair can be persuaded to incubate, as this allows the hen a period of rest from egg laying. If, for some reason, they should refuse to incubate, the nest box should be removed for a week or two, to give the hen sufficient time to recuperate, otherwise she may experience problems again if allowed to lay a further clutch so soon after egg-binding.

A hen that lays a *soft-shelled* egg while in the hospital cage must be rested. It is often possible to stop her laying further eggs, even when she has only laid one of a clutch, by taking away the nest box prior to releasing her back into her cage. Such a hen should be rested for at least three or four weeks and supplied daily with large quantities of flaked cuttlefish bone, chicken eggshell, and grit.

If a hen that has suffered from egg-binding is housed in either aviary or flight accommodation, and refuses to incubate after the clutch is completed, or lays a *soft-shelled* egg, then both she and her mate should be caught up and placed in a resting cage for at least three or four weeks. After this, the pair can again be released into the aviary or flight.

Hens of certain species of Australian finch, if egg-bound, will sit around, usually on the floor, with feathers fluffed and their eyes closed. Gouldians will always show such symptoms; however Bicheno Finch hens, when egg-bound, often remain in the nest and because of this the breeder may be unaware that the hen is experiencing difficulties. By the time the bird is found it is often too late for treatment to be effective.

EGGSHELL

A source of calcium which most Australian finches appear to relish is the shells from chickens' eggs. Empty, clean shells should first be placed in water which is heated and allowed to simmer for approximately two or three minutes. They can then be taken out and left to dry. Once dry they can be stored in a screw-top jar ready for use.

Crushed eggshells ready for feeding to Australian finches.

Gouldian Finches prefer the shell in large pieces and a pair will eat about a quarter of a large eggshell at one sitting. The remainder of the Australian finches prefer the shell to be in smaller portions and I usually take about a quarter of a shell in the palm of my hand and crush it slightly with my thumb. The pieces are then offered to the birds. The pieces of shell can be placed on top of the grit rather than directly on the floor. After 24 hours any uneaten pieces should be collected up and discarded, otherwise they may become soiled. Finches of all ages will take this shell, and it should be offered about every three or four days. Laying hens could be offered the shell more frequently.

EGGS (see NEST INSPECTION)

ELECTRICAL INSTALLATION

With any electrical installation the main requirements are safety of life and limb and the prevention of fire. If you have any doubts whatsoever about your competence in this area then do not attempt to carry out any form of electrical installation, but use this section as a specification for use by a fully qualified electrician.

Choices of components or equipment often depend partly upon cost. Therefore take the time to establish what is required, and always buy the best that you can afford. Always buy equipment made by firms whose names you recognize as being quality manufacturers. It is most important not to use unbranded equipment or components; your life could depend upon it.

Most countries throughout the world are harmonizing their electrical standards, thus making this section applicable in almost every country where Australian finches are kept. However, local differences are bound to occur. It is therefore wise to investigate the legal requirements before commencing work. Make sure that all of the work is carried out in a professional manner and is fully checked and tested before being brought into service.

Always use cables with the correct color insulation that is in force in your area. For instance, never use cable to carry live mains that is color coded for earth or protection, as this could have fatal consequences.

Most requirements will apply to either a birdroom or an outdoor aviary, with the exception that an outdoor aviary will require more in the way of weatherproofing, detailed inspection, and protection.

General requirements

The mains supply should be adequate to provide for all of your lights and heating, with power to spare. A local distribution board should be installed, either in the birdroom or aviary or very close to it, with separate fuses or circuit breakers for the lighting and heating circuits. A battery-powered mains-failure alarm should be connected to the outgoing side of the distribution board to warn of mains failure, thus enabling emergency measures to be taken quickly.

All wiring to sockets, switches, junction boxes, etc., should be neatly installed and protected either by being buried in the surface of the structure or run inside metal or plastic conduit. If buried in the structure, the runs should be marked in such a way as to prevent nails or screws from inadvertently being driven into the hidden cables. In general, this means that cables should be run in either true vertical or horizontal planes, and never at an angle. If this rule is adhered to, then only the ends of each run need to be marked, as the line of cable will be immediately apparent.

Never run cables under linoleum or, indeed, under any form of floor covering.

All metalwork, including wire mesh, must be bonded together, and grounded, using proper connectors, clamps, and cable.

Always arrange for power outlets to be placed as near as possible to the points where they are required. Likewise, any switches should be close to the doorways. Always remember that trailing leads are a real danger, both to yourself and to visitors. You may remember where the danger lies but your visitors will not, and if a cable is accidentally tripped over, wires can be ripped from plugs, thus causing the whole system to fuse, with disastrous consequences. Ensure that all switches, time switches, and thermostats are carefully located and firmly screwed into position. Also ensure that a complete mechanical and electrical inspection is made at least once each year.

Lighting

I have found the best form of general lighting to be the fluorescent lamp. The cheapest way of obtaining these is to purchase the complete unit, which comprises the fitting complete with control gear, starter switches, and lamps. There is little need for diffusers as, in general, they would not be required, as their only effect is to reduce the overall lighting level.

Always use more than one lighting unit as this improves the overall level and uniformity of the illumination. It also ensures that the failure of a single lamp does not plunge the birds into total darkness.

Always replace the fluorescent tubes when black bands form at the ends. This is an indication that you are not getting the light that you are paying for. Also, at this time

the risk of lamp failure is vastly increased, as is the risk of fire. It is also good practice to change any starter switches (if fitted) as a matter of course when you replace the tubes. I have also found that the best tubes to use are the triphosphor range, but failing the availability of these, any of the high-efficiency 'white' or 'daylight' types are a good substitute.

When using fluorescent tubes, it is not possible to fit a dimming device easily. Obviously birds cannot be plunged into complete darkness, and to enable any birds which have not gone to roost to do so after the main lights have been switched off, I have installed an 8-watt incandescent light bulb (of the type usually sold as a child's night light). This is switched on shortly before the main lights are due to be extinguished by the time switch. Then, first thing in the morning, upon entering the birdroom, I switch off the night light manually. As this type of lamp is so low-powered, it could, of course, be left on continuously, being replaced as and when required.

Heating

I have found that the best type of heater is the fan-assisted heater, as it provides warmth quickly and evenly. The heater should be controlled by a thermostat, the siting of which is most important, i.e., the thermostat should not be in any draft, nor in the airflow of the heater, nor where direct sunlight can fall upon it. The working of the thermostat should be checked from time to time, and it is a good idea to have a Min/Max (Sixes) thermometer in the

The ideal way to heat a birdroom is by installing an electric fan heater. Such a heater should be used in conjunction with a thermostat.

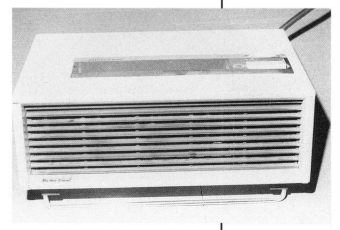

A thermostat is an essential part of the electrical installation in a birdroom.

A maximum/minimum thermometer enables you to monitor the temperature range.

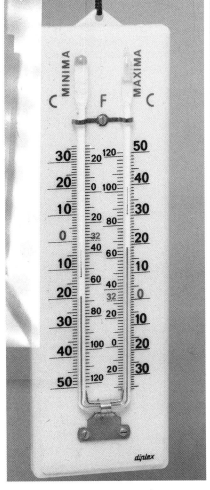

birdroom, thus enabling you to check for any excessive drift or deviation in temperature throughout each day.

Time switches

There are two types of time switch: The electrically powered version, derived from the old mechanical type of clock, with a rotating dial, and the digital nonmechanical type. The older type usually stops in a power failure and then resumes working on resumption of the supply, thus leaving the time switch out of line by the length of time that the power was off. This means that, in the event of a power failure, the switch would need to be checked and any drift in time corrected.

The digital types usually have a back-up battery built in, and therefore keep running even during a power failure. However, they must also be checked for drift from time to time, say, every three months or so. On the whole I prefer the digital type, as they are more reliable, although certain models can prove somewhat difficult to set up at first.

If you are subject to summer daylight saving times, you would have to reset the time switch at the start and finish of the saving period.

Spares

I keep a spare parts box for all my electrical bits and pieces, including

sockets, fuses, lamps, starter switches, and various other odds and ends. I have found in the past that the threads on electrical bolts appear to be different from any other kind of bolt. Therefore when any piece of equipment has failed and is beyond economical repair, I take it apart and any useful components, including nuts, bolts, and washers, are placed in my spare parts box before disposing of the rest of the equipment.

When first purchasing your equipment, give a thought to the spare parts situation and purchase at least one more complete unit than you require, together with spare starter-switch bases, and control gear, etc., thus obtaining compatibility from the outset. I have always found that the exact types of spare parts are almost impossible to obtain a few years after the original purchase, while if you have the correct spares at hand, a repair can be quickly and easily effected.

Always keep spare fluorescent tubes in the ratio of 50 percent of the lamps in service (i.e., if you are using four tubes, then keep at least two tubes as spares). Also keep starter switches in a 50 percent ratio, and all other spares as you feel necessary. Always replace your spares as and when you use them, using the failed component as a pattern.

Outdoor aviaries

There are two methods of running an electrical supply to an outdoor aviary, one being overhead, the other being underground.

All overhead cables should be supported from a noncorrosive metal wire, known as a catenary wire, which is securely fixed at each end. The supports should be regularly spaced, nylon or plastic straps being ideal for this. The cable should be PVC-sheathed and, if at all possible, ultra-violet stabilized. You may find that local laws require that the cable be a certain height from the ground. Even if there are no local requirements, you should ensure that the cable is well out of reach of children, and is high enough to enable ladders or such to be carried underneath it.

All underground cables should be protected by running them in a

duct. An inexpensive duct can be made from plastic waste pipe, using bends and connectors where necessary. The duct should be buried at least 50 cm (18 in) below the finished level, and the ends of the run marked. When the installation has been completed and tested, the ends of the duct must be sealed with some form of mastic to keep out moisture. If the end of the duct is within the enclosure of the aviary, then be sure that the sealant is nontoxic.

Any cable feeding an outdoor aviary should be protected at the end which is connected to the mains supply by means of a residual current circuit breaker. The outgoing side of the trip should be fitted with a battery-powered mains-failure alarm.

All cable used outside will need to be examined at regular intervals, and replaced as soon as any hairline cracking of the insulation or any other form of deterioration, such as a change in color, is noticed.

All lighting and heating for outdoor aviaries should be of a type suitable for use outside, and should be waterproof and noncorrosive. Supplementary heaters in the aviary shelter should be further protected by wire mesh to prevent the birds from coming into contact with them.

For further information see HEATING and LIGHTING.

EXHIBITING

At the present time, Australian finches can be exhibited as true pairs or as single birds of either sex. Many species are now virtually domesticated and, eventually, if these are declared by a leading body to be fully domesticated, then in all probability (as with Zebra and Society Finches) only true pairs of such species will be allowed on the show bench. As a good pair is invariably placed above a good single, it is preferable to exhibit true pairs if at all possible. However, both birds should be in show condition. If one is not, it would be prudent to exhibit only the bird which is, as a good single will take precedence over a pair if one member of the pair is mediocre.

No standards have yet been laid down for any species of Australian

A Black-headed Gouldian Finch pair shown in a desk-top cage.

finch, nevertheless pairs should be as well matched as possible. Birds with missing claws, or overgrown, chipped, or crossed beaks should not be used for exhibition. If shown in pairs, color variants should be of the same mutation. This means that not only should pairs of such mutations as the White-breasted Gouldian Finch be exhibited together, but the head color must also be taken into account, i.e., a Black-headed must be exhibited with a Black-headed, a Red-headed with a Red-headed, and so on. Subspecies should also be exhibited together, i.e., a White-rumped Bicheno Finch should be placed with another White-rumped, not with a Black-rumped.

Australian finches can be exhibited in a variety of show cages, although a recommended show cage is now available in the UK. The cage is what is known as the desk-pattern type and is 39 cm (15½ in) long by 32 cm (12½ in) high by 19 cm (7⅓ in) deep, sloping off to 12 cm (5 in) where the wire front angles inward. Two perches are fitted. A round access door is fitted on the right-hand side of the cage and a Zebra Finch type

of drinker is fitted to the inside of the front lower rail, with an access door which enables the birds to be watered without having to put one's hand inside the cage. The wire front is made of 12 mm (½ in) punch bar and is painted black. The inside of the cage is painted white, with the whole of the outside black. A similar show cage is currently under construction in the United States.

Seed containers are not normally used as they would tend to slide around the cage when it is being carried to and from the judging stand. Instead, the floor of the cage is covered with a layer of seed.

Personally, I feel the recommended show cage is too small for such species as Gouldian Finches and Long-tailed Grassfinches (also Heck's), as good-quality exhibition birds, with long tail-wires, would find it difficult to show themselves off to advantage due to their tail-wires continually coming into contact with the sides of the show cage. For these species I would recommend a desk-pattern type cage approximately 45 cm (18 in) long by 25 cm (10 in) wide and 30 cm (12 in) high. The recommended show cage has 12 mm (½ in) spacing between the bars of the wire front. This is suitable for most Australian finches, but I feel that for Bichenos the spacing should be, at the most, 9 mm (⅜ in), as a bird which became badly frightened could squeeze through the larger spacing.

No matter what size or type of show cage is used, no decoration should be added, as not only would it spoil the overall appearance of the exhibit, but if certain flowers and/or foliage were used, they could prove harmful to the birds if they attempted to eat them. Also, if the bird's plumage came into contact with such decorations, especially that of long-tailed species such as Gouldian Finches and Long-tailed Grassfinches, then their feathers could become disarranged, spoiling their chances of a red ticket.

Birds should be transported to and from exhibitions with care. During the colder months of the year the birds should not be subjected to great fluctuations in temperature. If they are to be transported by road, therefore, the vehicle should already be reasonably warm before the journey commences (see TRANSPORTATION).

FEATHERS, LOSS OF
Feather loss around the head, sometimes causing complete baldness, is a complaint often reported in the Gouldian Finch. Whether this is due to disease or stress is not certain. Over the years numerous remedies have been suggested, but none appear to have effected a permanent cure. Although affected birds look extremely unattractive, the lack of feathers does not appear to affect their health, and after the annual molt most will regain the lost feathers.

Many Gouldian Finch hens (rarely cocks), when rearing chicks, especially the second brood of the season, may lose facial and head feathers. This is not a cause for concern, as once the breeding season is over and the birds are allowed to rest and molt, all the missing feathers will be replaced.

Feather plucking in Australian finches is a vice which is rarely encountered. Star Finches, if housed under crowded conditions, may pluck each other, but a serious outbreak can easily be remedied by moving the birds to more spacious accommodation. Certain species may pluck out their own feathers, especially from the breast, if they

A Lutino Blue-faced Parrot Finch showing loss of feathers on its back — probably due to being plucked.

are not given sufficient nesting material. This, again, is not a serious problem and can easily be remedied by offering the birds extra material with which to build their nests.

FLOOR COVERING
The floor covering for cages can be newspaper, sand, sawdust, or peat. Personally, I have always used clean newspaper, as not only is this commodity cheap and commonly available, it is easily removed when soiled and is also easily disposed of. Six or seven layers of newspaper, placed on the floor of the cage, are sufficient to absorb feces, especially if the cage is cleaned thoroughly once a week. When birds are breeding, it may not be possible to clean out the cage quite as regularly. However, with pairs which are not easily stressed, it may prove possible to remove the top layer of newspaper from time to time. Once the chicks have fledged, one should take the opportunity at least to replace the newspaper, even if it is not possible to give the remainder of the cage a thorough cleaning.

The only problem I have encountered with newspaper is when certain cock birds insist on tearing strips from the paper and carrying these into the nest box, very often covering the eggs, and thus causing the pair to desert. Star Finch and Plum-headed Finch cocks are prone to this behavior and if they persist in it the breeder may have to remove the paper and resort to sand or such for the duration of the breeding season.

Rather than sand, I prefer to use stiff corrugated cardboard as a floor covering. I must emphasize that I only use it in a cage where the cock bird continually carries newspaper into the nest box, and then only for the duration of the incubation period. If it is possible to clean out the cage thoroughly shortly after the eggs have hatched, I then revert to newspaper, as it is only when eggs are in the nest that the problem of desertion may occur. Once the chicks have hatched, the cock and hen are usually too busy feeding their brood to have time to tear strips from the newspaper. Sand is no doubt used by many breeders as a cage floor covering. If one resides near the sea, then it is possible to

obtain sand for nothing. It should, however, be collected well away from the beach area and you must ensure it is clean and has not been contaminated by dogs or oil or polluted in any other way. However, even if I were able to obtain free supplies, I would not use sand as it is so difficult to remove from cages. Even when dropping trays are used, a certain amount will always fall between the tray and the cage sides. Also, when a bath is placed in the cage, the sand becomes extremely damp and, even in a warm room, does not dry out as easily as layers of newspaper.

Clean pine sawdust (from untreated wood) or peat are, I believe, used by some bird keepers as a floor covering, but both are easily blown about by the wing movements of the birds and this could cause food bowls to become covered, thus denying the birds access. Also, both sawdust and peat are extremely dusty, which must be something of a health hazard, not only to the birds but also to their owner!

Clean pine sawdust may prove suitable as a floor covering for an aviary shelter, especially if all feeding utensils are on a raised feeding station. Sand may also prove suitable here, but, unless it can be obtained free, it could prove expensive as a covering, especially if the shelter is a fairly large one. I cannot recommend peat at all, mainly because it is so dusty.

For an inside flight, I always use clean newspaper as a floor covering. It is cheap to provide, is easily removed, and, as already mentioned, is easily disposed of. Another excellent bedding is corn cob litter. It is a completely natural product made from clean, heat-dried corn cobs; it is biodegradable, will not cling, absorbs from the bottom upwards, and absorbs odors.

FOSTERING
The use of fosters for hatching eggs and rearing the young of Australian finches has been practiced since they were first known to aviculture. Nowadays this form of rearing is frowned upon by many enthusiasts as they believe that if Australian finches cannot be persuaded to hatch and rear their own young, then one

A cage used by the author for housing a breeding (or fostering) pair of Society (Bengalese) Finches.

should simply persevere until they will. However, I am not completely against the use of fosters as, under certain circumstances, a mutation or subspecies could be lost to aviculture if fosters were not employed. For instance, a few years ago I was fortunate enough to obtain a Black-rumped Bicheno Finch hen. At the time this subspecies was extremely rare in the United Kingdom and it was important that I obtain young from this bird. I paired her to a White-rumped cock bird, but although she would incubate and successfully hatch her eggs, she refused to rear the chicks. Because of this, I had no alternative but to place her eggs under a pair of Society Finches. For more details about the breeding history, see under INBREEDING.

The resulting young (which were visual White-rumped split for Black-rumped) were mated together and the original hen was mated back to one of her sons. I was eventually able to purchase some split Black-rumped birds from another breeder and, after persevering with these and my own-bred young for a couple of seasons, I was able to cease fostering out eggs and/or young and I now have an excellent stud of self-rearing Black-rumped Bicheno Finches.

The Society Finch is the most favored foster. Occasionally Zebra Finches are used, but they are not so accommodating as the Society. Also, such species as Bichenos may become imprinted on their Zebra Finch fosters, something which should be avoided at all costs.

It is possible that a strain of

Australian finches (of any species) which, over a period of years, were never allowed to incubate their eggs and/or rear their young, would eventually cease even to attempt incubation, but would continually lay clutch upon clutch of eggs. In spite of this, there is nothing detrimental in fostering out the occasional deserted eggs or young from pairs which have, in the past, successfully reared young themselves. However, Australian finches which continually refuse to incubate or attempt to rear their own young have no place in a stud belonging to a serious breeder.

In order to obtain as many chicks as possible each season, a chick or chicks can be transferred from one nest to another of the same species, rather than to Society Finches. Strict records would have to be maintained so that the breeder did not become confused. If at all possible, chicks should not be transferred until they have been closed-banded. Of course, chicks may require fostering out before they are old enough to be fitted with closed-bands. If this is the case, an attempt should be made to foster them with a pair (obviously of the same species) whose chicks will be different in some way.

The chicks to be transferred must be approximately the same age (give or take a few days) as those they are to be placed with, otherwise it is doubtful if the parent birds will accept them. If, for some reason, one has a pair of finches which have incubated a clutch of infertile eggs for the full term (or longer), it is often possible to foster newly hatched chicks onto them.

G

GENETICS

Genetics is the study of genes and how they affect the organism to which they belong. The first person to study this science was Gregor Mendel, who, while studying sweetpeas in his garden, noticed how various characteristics were passed on or lost through successive generations.

Unfortunately, many bird breeders 'switch off' the moment the word genetics is mentioned. This is most noticeable if, during a society meeting, the lecturer, who may have been listened to intently while he or she was talking about management and breeding, suddenly turns to the subject of color inheritance and, because of this, has to cover the basic rudiments relating to genetics. Within minutes, the once-attentive audience will begin to move around in their seats, feet will begin to be shuffled, and, if the lecturer presses on with the genetic theme, some members of the audience may openly begin to yawn!

It is not my intention to go into the subject of genetics in detail. However, throughout the text certain terms are used when discussing mutations and inheritance which I feel should be further explained.

The majority of mutations which have so far occurred in Australian finches are what are known as *recessive*. This means that should one of these color mutations be mated to a Normal (wild-colored) bird, the resulting young will all be Normal in color but will carry the mutant color in their genes. For example, if a Pied Star Finch is mated to a *pure* Normal Star, then the young from such a mating will be visual Normals but will be split for Pied. To obtain Pied birds from these split birds, you would have to mate them either to a visual Pied bird or to a split Pied (i.e., visual Normal split for Pied). However, the latter mating is not to be recommended as only a small percentage of Pied birds would be produced, with the remainder being either visual Normals split for Pied or pure Normals. It would be impossible to determine which were pure Normals and which were split birds.

On the other hand, if a split bird was mated to a Pied, the resulting young would be either Pied or visual Normals split for Pied. The mating of split to split is normally used only as a last resort, i.e., when the breeder has only split birds and is unable to obtain any visual mutants. There is an exception, however, in that White-rumped Bicheno Finches, which are split for Black-rumped, can be mated together as it would be possible to identify some of the split birds produced, as certain individuals would have black-and-white rumps. See BICHENO FINCH for a more detailed explanation of this.

A mutation which is *dominant* is completely the opposite to one which is recessive. For example, a Lilac-breasted Gouldian Finch is dominant to a White-breasted and if these mutations are mated together a percentage of Lilac-breasted young will be produced. A further example of this dominant character is the crested mutation in the Chestnut-breasted Finch. If crested birds are mated to non-crests, then a percentage of young with crests will be produced.

The majority of Normal (or wild-colored) birds are dominant to all color mutations and, if mated to the latter, then visual Normals split for the color mutation concerned will be produced. This is not strictly correct where the Gouldian Finch is concerned, however, as all three head colors are found in the wild, and in this species it is the Red-headed form which is dominant to both the Black-headed (cocks; see later) and the Orange- (Yellow-) headed (both cocks and hens).

Another term used when describing certain mutations is *sex-linked*. The correct term is 'recessive sex-linked' and it refers to circumstances where the sex of the bird has an influence on its color. For example, the Black-headed mutation in the Gouldian Finch is sex-linked so that if a Black-headed cock is mated to a Red-headed hen, then, of the resulting young, all the cocks

Star Finch (hen) —
Pied mutation.

will be visual Red-headed split for Black-headed and the hens will all be pure Black-headed. It is, in fact, impossible for a Black-headed bird of either sex to be split for Red-headed.

The term *split* describes a bird which, although of a certain color, is in fact 'carrying' in its genes a color which is not visually apparent. For example, if a dominant bird, such as a Red-headed (Normal) Gouldian Finch, is mated to a recessive, such as a Red-headed White-breasted, then the resulting young will all be visual Normal Red-headed Gouldians split for White-breasted. As a further example, if two recessive mutations are mated together, such as a Pied and a Yellow Star Finch, the young produced will be visual Normals but will be split (or will be carrying) both the Yellow and the Pied mutation.

There are now so many mutations appearing in Australian finches that it is difficult to keep up with them all. Color inheritance in certain mutations, such as the Black- and Orange-headed Gouldian Finches, and the White-breasted in all head colors, are well documented, but of the more recent mutations in this species, and the many mutations which are available in other Australian finch species, little has so far been recorded. For those who are keen to learn the intricacies of genetics, I would suggest they obtain a good book on the subject. The book need not necessarily be on genetics in birds, as even one which deals with genetics in general would help the reader to understand the subject more easily.

GOULDIAN FINCH (*Chloebia gouldiae*) (color photos on pages 18–19, 22–23, 26–27, 30–31)
The approximate overall length of the cock Gouldian Finch is 127 mm (5 in). Hens, due to their shorter

An immature
Gouldian Finch
(cock) at eight
weeks of age.

tail wires, are usually a little smaller, although, bodywise, both sexes are about the same size. Adult cocks (Red-headed form) have the lores, cheeks, ear coverts, forehead, and sinciput dull scarlet, bordered by a narrow line of black, widening into a black patch on the upper throat, and followed by a band of turquoise, broader on the occiput. The general color above, including the upper-wing coverts and inner secondaries, is grass-green. The nape is apple-green. The foreneck and chest are purple, margined below with a narrow yellowish-orange band. The breast, sides of the body, and abdomen are rich yellow, turning to white on the center of the lower abdomen and under-tail coverts. The beak is grayish white (pearly white when in breeding condition), tipped with red.

Adult hens are similar to the cock but noticeably paler on the breast and underparts. The beak usually turns blackish when in breeding condition.

The Black-headed form is similar to the Red-headed, but has the regions of the head black instead of dull scarlet.

The Orange-headed form

Gouldian Finch
chicks at nine days
of age.

has the red areas replaced with orange.

At one time the range of this species extended across a wide area of northern Australia. However, not only has its range severely contracted, its numbers have also declined rapidly, particularly over the past 20 years or so. Research is at present being carried out regarding the rapid decline of the Gouldian Finch in the wild. Although not as yet conclusive, evidence of Air-sac Mite (*Sternostoma tracheacolum*) found in Gouldians taken from the wild could be one of the causes of the rapid drop in numbers (see MITE).

Without doubt, the Gouldian is the most popular of all the Australian finches. This is understandable, as not only is it highly colorful (being considered by many to be the most beautiful of all the Estrildids), but for the more experienced bird keeper it usually proves fairly easy to breed, especially when housed as individual pairs in roomy cages.

Sexing adults is easy because, as mentioned earlier, although the hen is similar in plumage to the cock, she is noticeably paler on the breast and underparts. In the Red- and Orange-headed form, the head coloring in a hen is not as vivid as that of the cock.

Of the three head colors in the Gouldian Finch, red, black, and orange (the latter often being referred to as yellow), the Red-headed is the most numerous in captivity, followed by the Black-headed. The Orange-headed, although by no means rare, is not as numerous as the other two.

Mention should be made of the rather dull-colored plumage of immature Gouldian Finches, as a newcomer to the species may be somewhat surprised when seeing a newly fledged bird for the first time (see IMMATURE PLUMAGE).

The majority of Gouldian Finch enthusiasts house their breeding pairs in cages. In most temperate regions this type of accommodation is almost obligatory, especially during the colder months of the year. In areas where conditions are more favorable, Gouldians can be successfully housed in aviaries. However, as the majority of breeders wish to linebreed their birds, and as there is little or no control over aviary birds, no doubt the serious breeder (no matter where he or she lives) will prefer to cage-breed, especially if the aim is to produce mutations or head colors.

Of all the Australian finches, the Gouldian has the most pronounced breeding pattern. If it is not allowed to carry out its full cycle, it is possible that a breeding attempt will fail.

To someone who is not conversant with the breeding behavior of the Gouldian, certain aspects can prove somewhat worrying. It is therefore beneficial for a potential breeder to understand the cycle fully, as not only will this eliminate the need for concern, it should enable the breeder to produce more chicks each season.

The birds must be in breeding condition before attempts are made to place breeding pairs together. When in breeding condition, cock birds usually have almost white beaks, with only the tips being colored. Those cock birds which are eager to nest will be seen to sing regularly and will call incessantly to the hens, the latter usually answering them. Hens which are in breeding condition usually have an almost black beak. However, this is not always so and a more obvious sign is when the hens can be seen to be 'heavy,' with a pronounced rise to the rump and with the tail held in a downward position.

Incubation does not commence until the final egg of the clutch is laid. Both birds may sit in the nest box during the day (either individually or together), but until the clutch is completed, they will leave the nest to sleep on a perch. As soon as the hen is seen to remain on the nest during the night, one can assume that incubation has begun. Incubation takes from 14 to 16 days, according to how 'tightly' the birds sit. The hen does most of the incubating and it is invariably she who sits at night, the cock taking over at first light and again for short periods throughout the day. One can usually tell when the chicks have hatched by the behavior of the parent birds, as they will change over duties more frequently. However, it is still the hen who covers the chicks at night.

When the chicks are ten days of age, the parents cease to brood. Occasionally one comes across a pair which will cover the chicks for longer than ten days, but this is most certainly the exception rather than the rule. If it is intended to closed-band the chicks, then this is the time to do so, as well-fed Gouldian Finch chicks are ready for this at ten days of age.

The chicks leave the nest at approximately 25 days of age and can be weaned within five to six weeks. By this time they should be feeding themselves, taking little if any food directly from the parent birds.

There is much variation in the length of time it can take for Gouldians to molt from immature to full adult plumage. Many young birds complete their first molt within a four-month period, whereas others can take almost a year. In extreme cases, a period of 18 months has been recorded. If a bird of 12 months or more has not molted into full adult plumage, complications may arise. Such birds, due solely to their age, may be in breeding condition and, if not used in the breeding pen, they will often refuse to molt, maybe for many months. If used for breeding, they will, when breeding is over,

immediately commence to molt and only then will they attain full adult plumage.

Despite this, I am totally against the use of birds in immature plumage being used for breeding. Such birds will often go down to nest and rear young successfully, but the progeny from these birds are usually also slow to molt into adult plumage. If one mates a bird that is in full adult plumage to one that is not, many of the young (usually of the same sex as the slow-molting bird) will also fail to molt out in a reasonable time. Because of this, I would suggest that slow-molting birds (i.e., those that do not attain full, or almost full, adult plumage within approximately six months of hatching), rather than be used for breeding, be passed on to someone who requires the birds solely as an attraction in a mixed flight or aviary.

Mutations

Although there are three head colors in the (wild) Gouldian Finch (red, black, and orange), only two of these are classed as head-color mutations, namely the black and the orange, the red being regarded as Normal.

Gouldian Finches. From left to right: Black-headed (hen), Red-headed (cock) and young (hen) in the final stages of molt from immature to adult plumage.

Chest-band mutations

At present, there are three chest-band mutations, where the purple of the Normal is replaced with either white, lilac (given the name rose in the USA), or blue. The White-breasted first appeared in Australia in 1954 and in South Africa in the late 1950s. However, serious attempts at reproducing the mutation were not carried out until 1965, when F. Barnicoat (South Africa) obtained two cock birds. All the White-breasteds held in captivity have originated from those originally owned by Mr. Barnicoat.

The Lilac-breasted appeared in the United Kingdom in 1978. At first it was reasonably popular (mainly with a small number of breeders in the Midlands area), but the mutation has, up to the present time, never become universally popular and, with more colorful mutations appearing, the Lilac-breasted may eventually disappear if concerted efforts are not made to keep it going.

The Blue-breasted first appeared in the USA and is now fairly widely bred there. It has been imported into the UK but, as yet, is far from established.

Blue-backed

The Blue-backed, or Blue, as the name suggests, is blue wherever the Normal Gouldian is green. As this mutation lacks the ability to manufacture lutein, all the other colors are also diluted, hence the Red- and Orange-headed appear as 'yellow,' with the yellow of the abdomen paler than in the Normal. Unlike the Yellow and Dilute mutations (see later), the Blue-backed is able to produce melanin. Therefore the head color (in the Black-headed) is not affected and the flight and tail feathers (in all head colors) are as in the Normal.

Yellow (Dilute Yellow)

The Yellow is a most striking mutation, with the areas of plumage which are green in the Normal being yellow or, in the dilute form, lime-green. The blue areas are reduced to near white in the Yellow and to pale sky-blue in the dilute form. Red- and

Orange-head colors are as in the Normal, but 'Black-headed' birds have pale yellowish-gray heads in the yellow phase and pale slate-gray heads in the dilute form.

Dilute

This mutation is somewhat variable in appearance, with the body color ranging from fawn to washed-out green. There is, however, a more attractive mutation, referred to as the 'Australian' Dilute, where the wings and back are cream with the remainder of the plumage appearing Normal, other than the black bib and the head band, which is white. Black-headed birds have a gray head and, as with the blue mutation, are most unattractive.

All these mutations are available in the Purple- (Normal) or the White-breasted phase but, as far as I am aware, none are yet available in the Lilac-breasted form. There is much discussion as to how certain mutations can be perpetuated, but the actual genetics of all but the three head colors and the White- and Lilac-breasted have yet to be fully determined.

GREEN FOOD

Green food is of great benefit to Australian finches since it forms a valuable source of Vitamins A and D (deficient in dry seeds), proteins, and minerals. It also helps to provide variety in the diet and is especially important as a rearing food.

Most Australian finch species will eat some form of green food, especially when they are rearing chicks, and even those individuals who have in the past refused to take green food can often be persuaded to do so if housed for a short while with other birds that eat it regularly.

For those aviculturists who reside in rural areas, it is often possible to collect certain foods from the wild. However, those living in more built-up areas may find it impossible to do so. If green food is collected from the wild, it must be gathered in an area which has not been fouled by cats or dogs and has not been sprayed with insecticides; it should never be collected from roadside verges as such areas are bound to be contaminated by fumes from vehicle exhausts.

Personally, I have never used green food collected from the wild as I feel that one can never be absolutely sure it has not been polluted in some way. I prefer to offer my birds thoroughly washed lettuce; indeed this is the only green food I have ever given to my birds. The birds relish it and, once it has been thoroughly washed under a running cold-water tap, I feel it is entirely safe to use. Only the green outer leaves are offered to the birds, as little interest is shown in the whitish inner leaves.

For caged birds and those housed in indoor flights, green food can be offered by placing it in a clip of the type used to hold cuttlefish bone, and attaching it to the cage front or wire of the flight. Aviary birds should not have their green food attached to the wire of the outside flight, as if they spend too much time near the wire, they could encourage cats. I would suggest, therefore, that green food supplied to aviary birds either be placed on the feeding station inside the shelter or hung near a perch in the center of the outside flight.

Although I supply only lettuce to my birds, other cultivated green foods, such as spinach and cabbage, can be offered.

Whatever type of green food is offered, any left uneaten must be removed each evening, otherwise it may begin to decay and in such a condition could prove a serious health hazard to your birds.

GRIT

Grit is an essential part of the diet of all birds that consume seeds. When ingested into the bird's gizzard, the sharp edges of the pieces of grit help to grind down the seeds, after which the grit slowly dissolves in the acids of the stomach, thus releasing valuable minerals into the bird's system.

Grit also provides the basic minerals for the production of eggshell, and therefore breeding hens will require a plentiful supply both before and during the breeding season.

The grit most favored by Australian finches is the type known as mineralized grit, which also contains various trace elements. To add variety, limestone grit and oystershell should also be offered. Both limestone and oystershell are available in different grades and only the smallest grade (usually referred to as 'fine') should be offered to Australian finches, as the coarser grades are too large for them.

So important is grit to the health and well-being of Australian finches that it is essential that all three forms are made available at all times. For aviary birds, each type of grit should be offered separately in shallow dishes, preferably in the shelter.

For caged birds, the three types of grit can be placed together in a small dish on the floor of the cage, well away from perches. Birds usually show a marked preference for certain portions of the grit supplied and because of this any grit which remains uneaten is most probably unsuitable for their needs. Every week, therefore, whether or not all the contents have been eaten, the dish (or dishes) should be emptied, washed thoroughly, and replenished.

Mineralized grit (left) and oystershell grit.

H

HANDLING

Birds should only be handled when it is absolutely necessary. All, with the exception of pet birds, loathe to be caught and touched. However, there comes a time when handling is necessary. Small-sized birds, such as Australian finches, are best held with the back in the palm of your hand, with the head projecting between the first finger and thumb, which grip the neck firmly but not tightly. The bird should then nestle snugly in the hand and can also be gently restrained by gripping the legs between your last two fingers (see CATCHING).

HEATING

If a mixed collection of Australian finches is housed in the same quarters, then the heat provided must be in relation to the species which requires the highest temperature. Gouldian Finches enjoy a relatively high temperature in the wild and captive birds require a temperature of around 18°C (64°F). Most other species can be kept successfully at slightly lower temperatures, especially out of the breeding season. One reads of Australian finches being kept without heat of any kind throughout the year, but it is not a practice I would recommend in most temperate areas.

The ideal way in which to heat a birdroom is by using a good-quality electric fan heater in conjunction with a reliable thermostat. Birds housed permanently in aviaries should be provided with a heated shelter to which they can retire should they feel the need. It may not be possible to use a fan heater under these conditions. If this is the case, then electric tubular heaters would have to be employed. These are not as efficient as fan heaters and one may have to install a number of tubes if the correct temperature is to be maintained. (See ELECTRICAL INSTALLATION and TEMPERATURE.)

HECK'S GRASSFINCH (*Poephila acuticauda hecki*) (color photos on pages 83, 86–87)

As mentioned elsewhere (see LONG-TAILED GRASSFINCH), the Heck's Grassfinch is a subspecies of the Long-tail. In appearance it is identical to the latter, except for its sealing-wax-red beak. Housing, dietary, and breeding requirements are exactly the same as described for the Long-tail.

It appears that the Heck's is rare in aviculture in Australia and, as yet, in the United States. In the United Kingdom, however, it is one of the most (if not the most) commonly kept Australian finches and large numbers are bred each year; so many, in fact, that breeders often find difficulty in selling surplus young. It is the ideal species for the newcomer, being hardy and easy to breed. The only problem is the difficulty in sexing. However, if the procedures described under the Long-tailed Grassfinch are adhered to, even sexing should not cause too much difficulty.

The Heck's will go to nest and successfully rear young in a cage, aviary, or indoor flight. It is a hardy species and will winter successfully in an outdoor aviary as long as a draft-proof, warm shelter is provided. Heck's should not be allowed to breed in outdoor aviaries during the winter months, as losses may occur through hens becoming egg-bound.

Unfortunately, there are many 'mongrel' Heck's to be seen in the UK at the present time. Also, through indiscriminate mating of poor-quality stock, many Heck's can now be seen which are not only poorly colored but also undersized. The true Heck's is a fairly large, robust bird with smooth feathering, attractive markings (when clearly defined), and a brilliant red beak. 'Mongrel' stock has been brought about by the indiscriminate mating of Heck's to Long-tails. The Heck's is dominant to the Long-tail and the progeny from such a mating usually have orange-colored beaks instead of the deep red of pure-bred birds. More and more birds with orange-colored beaks are seen nowadays, not because they have been mated to Long-tails (the latter now being so scarce in the UK that few are seen), but because no consideration for beak

Young Heck's
Grassfinch —
White mutation.

color has been taken into account when pairing up stock. Also, the appearance of several mutations (see below) has not helped matters as many, due to their genetic make-up, do not have the true red beak of the normal Heck's and, when such birds are mated to pure Heck's, the beak color of the resulting young deteriorates.

At present there are at least five mutations in the Heck's Grassfinch. Some are so numerous that, unlike the majority of mutations, they do not command a higher price than the Normal bird. Indeed, if deterioration continues in the Normal Heck's, I can envisage a good, well-colored Normal bird being more expensive than certain mutations.

The Fawn mutation is very common. Small, poorly marked specimens abound and if it is to retain its attraction, then selective breeding for size and color must be introduced. The White mutation is not seen in great numbers, although it is certainly well established. Like the Fawn, it

would benefit from selective breeding. Cream Heck's are extremely attractive and if large well-colored birds continue to be produced, I cannot see the mutation losing favor.

The Pied Heck's, if well marked with pied areas forming approximately 50 percent of the overall color, can prove to be most attractive. At present in the UK it is the least available of the mutations and, because of this, it commands the highest price.

A practice which is to be abhorred is the mating of mutation Heck's to Black-throated (Parson) Finches. It appears that this is carried out extensively in Europe and on a much lesser scale in the UK also. Such indiscriminate matings were no doubt carried out to enable mutations which appeared in the Heck's, but not in the Black-throated, to be transposed into the latter. However, all that such matings have in fact achieved is to produce 'mongrel' birds which are typical of neither species, i.e., 'Black-throated

Grassfinches (1)

Long-tailed Grassfinch (cock). One of the most elegant of Australian finches, the Long-tailed (with the yellow beak) is somewhat rare in the UK. However, in Australia and the USA it is well established. The species is easy to care for and breed and is ideally suited both to the beginner and the more experienced aviculturist.

Masked Grassfinch. The Masked is one of the most difficult species to sex by visual means. It is not particularly popular, due, no doubt, to the problems one has in locating true pairs. As it is also difficult to breed, the Masked cannot be recommended to the complete newcomer to Australian finches. However, to the keen enthusiast, who has experience with other Australian finch species, the Masked presents a challenge well worth taking up.

Black-throated Finch.

This species is often referred to as the Parson Finch. It is free-breeding and large numbers are bred each year, both in outdoor aviaries and in roomy cages in birdrooms. Due to its lack of tail wires, it is not as elegant as the Long-tailed Grassfinch (and Heck's), which it resembles except for its black beak. Nevertheless, it is a most attractive species and is ideal for the newcomer as well as the more experienced aviculturist.

Heck's Grassfinch.

In the UK the Heck's is the most widely bred of all the Australian finches. It is easy to cater for and can be housed in outdoor aviaries, indoor flights or in roomy cages in a birdroom.

It is a subspecies of the Long-tailed Grassfinch. Whereas the latter has a yellow beak, the Heck's beak, in a good specimen, is sealing-wax-red. The Heck's is dominant to the Long-tailed and if it is mated to the latter, all progeny will have red beaks.

Finches' with reddish-colored beaks and rudimentary tail wires, and 'Heck's' with very short, almost nonexistent tail wires. So interbred are many of these birds that it would prove impossible to obtain pure strains of either species from them.

HOSPITAL CAGE

There is little doubt that a hospital cage is ideal when one is confronted with a hen which is egg-bound (see EGG-BINDING). However, this is the only time I would use such a cage. An ailing bird can often be brought back to health with the application of heat alone and while I have no doubt that many have been saved by placing them in a hospital cage, such cages almost certainly cause stress and this factor alone can easily kill a bird. Under such circumstances, rather than use a hospital cage, I would suggest one employ an infrared lamp. Such a

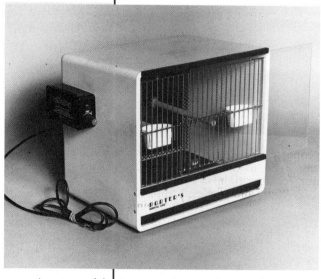

A commercial hospital cage, fully fitted, and with sliding glass front. This cage is thermostatically controlled.

lamp can be attached to the bars of a flight or breeding cage and the ailing bird can then perch near to, or move away from, the heat source as and when it wishes (see INFRARED LAMP).

If you do decide to use a hospital cage in an attempt to bring an ailing bird back to health, then the temperature of the cage must be kept at a constant 30°C (86°F) until the bird appears to be well again. The temperature of the cage should then be lowered gradually until it is at the same level as that at which the bird is normally kept. The bird

can then be released back into its quarters.

HUMIDITY

The majority of Australian finches are believed to require a humidity level of around 70 percent if they are to remain in good health. If birds are allowed to bathe regularly, this action alone should create sufficient humidity. For those who feel their birds may be suffering from a dry atmosphere, a humidifier could be installed. Alternatively, an open dish of water could be kept permanently in the birdroom, preferably near to, or directly above, the heater.

To find out the actual humidity level in your birdroom, a humidity gauge should be placed in a convenient position in the room. These gauges can usually be purchased from a shop dealing in gardening requisites.

HYGIENE

Hygiene is an essential part of good management. If neglected, it could result in poor breeding returns and even death among your stock. Regular cleaning of all accommodation is essential. All feeding utensils (including the containers in which foods are stored) should also receive regular cleaning, as should nest boxes, perches, etc. Obviously, when birds are incubating or rearing young, it may not prove possible to clean their living quarters as regularly as you would like (especially if they are housed in cages). Nevertheless, the moment the opportunity arises (such as when the young have fledged), the birds' accommodation should be cleaned. If housed in a cage, as soon as the young are removed, the cage and the nest box should be given a thorough cleaning before the birds are allowed to nest again. See NEST BOXES for further information on nest-box hygiene.

I

IMMATURE PLUMAGE IN AUSTRALIAN FINCHES

(see page 88.)

IMPRINTING

Filial imprinting, i.e., the imprinting of young birds on their parents, is an important part of keeping the family group together. However, the process can also have profound effects on an individual when it reaches maturity. This is the case in sexual imprinting. The developing youngster sexually imprints on its parents and, on reaching maturity, will normally mate only with a member of that species. Obviously there are exceptions to the rule, otherwise hybrids between different species of birds would never be produced.

Normally this phenomenon goes unnoticed because young are reared by, and imprint on, their natural parents. Subsequently, they mate with their own kind. However, when fosters are used for the hatching and/or rearing of deserted eggs or young, problems may arise.

Investigation was carried out by Klaus Immelmann (*Proceedings of the XVth International Ornithological Congress*, 1972, pp. 316–338), with regard to imprinting in the Society Finch and the Zebra Finch. Immelmann found that cock Zebra Finches that were reared under Society Finches imprinted on their foster parents and, on reaching maturity, behaved as if they were Societys.

Unfortunately, little or no research has been carried out with regard to imprinting in Australian finches, other than in the Zebra Finch.

From my own observations, I believe that it is possible for certain individuals to become imprinted on their foster parents. Therefore, if Society Finches are used for rearing Australian finch chicks, it is essential the chicks be removed to a cage well away from the foster parents the moment they are seen to be independent. Also, it is preferable to house young stock with their own kind only. To mix youngsters of different species could mean that certain individuals may become song-imprinted on the species with which they are housed. Species which are known to peer (i.e., individuals which stand close beside, or in front of, a singing bird, peering intently at the latter and giving the impression that they are listening to the song), may imitate the song of the species with which they are housed. This could cause complications when such birds are used for breeding.

Cocks of certain species (such as Star Finches) commence singing at an early age. If it is found that they are attempting to reproduce the song of their foster parents, rather than their own natural song, they should be housed with an adult cock bird of their own species which is in full song. Caught in time, the young bird or birds should begin to imitate the song of the cock bird and, eventually, cease to use the song of their foster parents.

INBREEDING

Inbreeding is usually defined as the mating of closely related birds with the specific aim of fixing desirable properties and traits. This is generally achieved by mating father to daughter, mother to son, or brother to sister. If reasonable and properly applied inbreeding is employed, then the desirable traits may well be attained. However, if unskillfully and carelessly applied, inbreeding can fix more bad points than it can good ones.

The original pair(s) which are initially mated in an inbreeding program must possess the properties and traits you are trying to establish. Correct inbreeding not only produces birds which are of good quality but also birds which are capable of breeding youngsters as good as, or better than, themselves, something which the continuous mating of unrelated stock (see OUTBREEDING) cannot be relied upon to do.

Consistent and intensive inbreeding should only be undertaken by those who thoroughly understand what they are about. Novices owning small studs of birds of only moderate quality should not attempt to

Grassfinches (2)

Heck's Grassfinch (hen) with one of her chicks – White mutation. The chick is on the left. This is an attractive mutation, although, as can be seen, certain specimens lack the deep red beak of the Normal Heck's. This is a fault which can be rectified by mating such birds to well-colored Normals. The resulting progeny, which will be visual Normals split for White, could then be mated back to white birds.

Heck's Grassfinch – Fawn mutation. This mutation is sex-linked and Fawns can be obtained from mating two together, when all Fawns will be produced, or by mating a Fawn cock to a Normal hen, which will produce visual Normal cocks split for Fawn and Fawn hens.

Heck's Grassfinch (cock) – Cream mutation.
A fine example of the Cream mutation, this bird has good overall body color and excellent beak color.

Heck's Grassfinch (hen) – Cream mutation.
Although Heck's (both in the Normal and in the various mutations) are often difficult to sex visually, if this bird is compared with the cock (above), it will be seen that the throat patch and flank markings are less pronounced. The beak color is also less intense.

Heck's Grassfinch – White mutation.
This bird has an extremely well-colored beak. See the caption on page 86 (top).

IMMATURE PLUMAGE IN AUSTRALIAN FINCHES

Species	Description
Beautiful Firetail	Duller in color than adult, being basically gray. Beak black.
Bicheno Finch	More brown on upperparts than adults and with less pronounced markings, those of the wings being buffish or dull white and barred rather than spotted. Breast bands are usually present, however some immature birds may lack either one or both, and have the whole of the underparts grayish-white, darker on the breast which may vary from gray to pale gray. Beak, legs, and feet blackish.
Black-throated Finch	Overall duller in color than adults, with the much reduced throat patch grayish-black.
Blue-faced Parrot Finch	Uniform dull green, paler on the underparts. Beak not as dark as in the adult bird.
Chestnut-breasted Finch	Upperparts olive-brown; breast brownish-buff with remainder of underparts pale buff.
Crimson Finch	Upperparts, including sides of head, dull grayish-brown. Upper-tail coverts and outer margins of secondaries and tail feathers dull crimson. Throat and upper breast pale brown; lower breast and abdomen fulvous-brown. Beak blackish.
Diamond Firetail	Back and wings dull olive-brown; rump and upper-tail coverts crimson; tail brownish-black; head, cheeks, and ear coverts grayish-olive; sides of foreneck and flanks olive-brown with wide bars of grayish-white and a small amount of blackish-brown feathers which have white subterminal spots; remainder of underparts white. Beak gray-black.
Gouldian Finch	Upperparts mainly olive-green suffused with gray around the head and neck. Underparts paler, turning to white on lower abdomen and under-tail coverts.
Long-tailed Grassfinch	Overall duller in color than adults, with the throat patch dull gray and much more reduced. Beak and legs black.
Masked Grassfinch	Overall color dull brown, paler on underparts. Facial mask smaller than in adult and gray rather than black. Beak and legs black.
Painted Firetail	Dull-colored, with no scarlet on head or throat. Beak black.
Pictorella Finch	Dark brownish-gray, lighter on the underparts. Beak brownish-black.
Plum-headed Finch	Upperparts dull olive-brown without head or chin markings. Underparts grayish-white without barring. Beak black.

Star Finch (hen) with fledgling.

Red-browed Finch	General color more dull than adults, with mainly dusky olive-green upperparts and smoky-brown underparts. Rump is dull crimson and there are no eye flashes. Beak is black.
Red-eared Firetail	Dull brownish-gray with no red ear patch or white spotting on flanks. Beak black.
Star Finch	Upperparts dull olive-brown; head and facial area grayish; underparts pale olive turning to white on lower abdomen and under-tail coverts. Beak black. This species also has a sub-adult plumage phase. (See individual species for full details.)
Yellow-rumped Finch	Upperparts and throat dark brown; breast pale gray with remainder of underparts grayish-buff.

inbreed extensively until they have gained experience, but should rely on purchased birds to help bring their stud up to the standard they require (see OUTBREEDING).

There are those who are totally against any form of inbreeding, as they feel that it is 'unnatural' for closely related birds to be mated together; others insist that inbreeding reduces vigor in one's stock. Taking the first point, inbreeding almost certainly occurs among gregarious birds in the wild. That it is totally uncontrolled is obvious, but the reason it does not

Grassfinches (3)

Black-throated Finch – Fawn mutation. As with all the birds depicted under the heading Grassfinches 3, this bird has a reddish-colored beak. Pure-bred Black-throated Finches should have black beaks and it is obvious that the three mutations illustrated have Heck's Grassfinch blood in their make-up. It is also obvious that the Heck's is not only dominant to the Long-tailed Grassfinch (with the yellow beak), but to the Black-throated Finch also.

Black-throated
Finch (cock) –
Cream mutation.

Black-throated
Finch (hen) –
Cream mutation.

lead to deterioration in wild birds (as would uncontrolled inbreeding in captive birds) is because among wild birds only the fittest survive to reproduce. This is not the case with birds bred in captivity, where, due to the conditions under which they are kept, those which are of poor quality can still survive.

With regard to the second point, if the birds produced from inbreeding lack vigor, then it is not necessarily because they are from closely related stock, but may be because the original stock lacked vigor in the first place. As mentioned earlier, inbreeding not only brings out the good points, it can also emphasize the bad points. If you mate closely related birds which are lacking in vigor, then, obviously, this fault will be emphasized in the youngsters produced. However, if unrelated birds which are lacking in vigor are mated together, they also produce youngsters which are lacking in vigor. It is not inbreeding which causes lack of vigor, but the way in which you pair your birds together that causes problems to arise.

In certain cases you may have to resort to inbreeding, even if you are one of those breeders who is normally against the practice. To give an example, a few years ago I purchased a Black-rumped Bicheno hen. At the time this race was extremely scarce in the UK and the hen was the first Black-rumped I had ever seen. She was rather undersized, but as she was a Black-rumped I decided to purchase her. Eventually I mated her to a White-rumped cock of my own breeding. He was of excellent size and quality (traits completely missing in the hen) and the resulting young, although not as large as their father, were a vast improvement on their rather small mother.

Being unable to find another Black-rumped Bicheno (of either sex), I had no option but to pair not only brother to sister, but also one of the best of the young cocks to his mother. By using only the best of the youngsters for breeding, this meant that with each generation size and vigor increased also. From the various matings a number of Black-rumped birds were also produced. This technique was also combined with that of fostering, as described under FOSTERING. I eventually located a

breeder who not only had some split Black-rumped birds (see BICHENO FINCH; also GENETICS) but was willing to sell me a cock and a hen. I paired these with birds of my own breeding and within three years I had an excellent stud of Black-rumped birds without having to buy in any more birds. If I had not resorted to inbreeding, I would not now have such a good stud of Black-rumped Bicheno Finches.

INDOOR FLIGHTS

Indoor flights may prove suitable for colony-breeding certain species of Australian finches. However, such a flight would take up as much

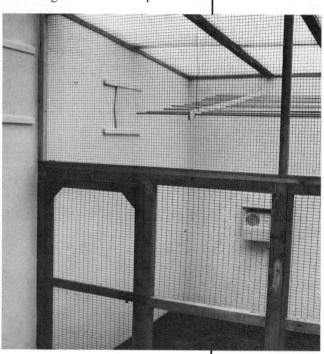

space as a block of cages and, as there is more control over caged birds, I see little advantage in keeping birds in such accommodation.

A reasonably large flight would no doubt prove suitable for molting and growing on young stock (or for resting adults), but the former would need to be carefully watched when first released into the flight, especially if they had been cage-bred, to ensure that they found the food and water containers easily.

Species such as Bicheno Finches, which are somewhat weak flyers, would require an abundance of thin, natural perches placed around the flight to enable the birds to move around freely.

An indoor flight like this is suitable only for resting adults or for molting and growing on young stock. The perching arrangements would not be suitable for Bicheno Finches.

An infrared lamp attached to a cage.

L

INFRARED LAMP

As mentioned under HOSPITAL CAGE, an ailing bird can often be brought back to health through the application of heat alone. The best source is undoubtedly an infrared lamp. Various types are available, but the one most suited to the aviculturist's needs is the dull emitter with a ceramic element. It has no light (which is ideal at night as it allows the ailing bird to sleep), is unaffected by water splashes, is virtually unbreakable and, if handled with reasonable care, has an extremely long life. Also, the low filament temperature eliminates fire risk.

The lamp can be fastened to the front of an ordinary breeding or flight cage with a perch placed immediately in front of the lamp. Another perch should also be fixed well away from the lamp to enable the bird to move away from the heat source should it so desire.

The advantage of such a lamp over a hospital cage is that not only can an ailing bird be housed in a cage similar to that which it has been used to, but food and water can also be supplied in exactly the same way as for birds in full health. A bathing saucer could even be placed in the cage. All of this helps to alleviate stress, thus ensuring that the ailing bird has a reasonable chance of recovery.

LADY GOULD FINCH
(see GOULDIAN FINCH)

LIGHTING

Australian finches require approximately 15 hours of light each day, especially when breeding. As many enthusiasts breed from their birds during the winter months, it is essential that lighting is installed, no matter what type of accommodation the birds are housed in.

Fluorescent tubes are ideal; they provide almost shadow-free illumination and, if installed correctly, they should throw out light which reaches all parts of the birdroom. The lights in my birdroom are set (by a time switch) to come on at 6 A.M. and to go off at 9:30 P.M.

Such species as Gouldian Finches, which are flock birds, are prone to night fright. To combat this, it is preferable if a night light is installed. This need only be a small-wattage bulb, which can be left burning during the night, thus enabling any bird which, through disturbance, has left its perch to be able to find the perch again easily.

A night light is beneficial to birds housed in aviaries, especially if one is plagued by cats. (See also ELECTRICAL INSTALLATION.)

LINEBREEDING

The term linebreeding is regarded by many to be synonymous with inbreeding. However, whereas the latter term is normally used to describe the mating together of very closely related birds, linebreeding is usually considered to be the mating together of more distantly related stock.

Whatever term is used, the same principles apply (see INBREEDING).

LIVE FOOD

Although the majority of Australian finches will successfully raise their young on a diet of seed alone, many appreciate live food at such times, and certain species may have difficulty in completing the actual rearing of chicks if some form of

Australian Mannikins

Chestnut-breasted Finch. Sometimes given the name Chestnut-breasted Mannikin, this species is probably the most popular of the Australian mannikins, and is certainly the one most often bred. However, as with all of the Australian mannikins, the Chestnut-breasted is not widely kept, and even in its country of origin numbers are fairly low.

Yellow-rumped Finch.
   Of all the Australian mannikins, the Yellow-rumped is the least popular among aviculturists. It appears that numbers are low, not only in aviculture, but in the wild also. If the species is to remain available to future Australian finch enthusiasts, then a concerted captive-breeding program is required.
   The species is difficult to sex by visual means, although cock birds can be identified by their song which, in young birds molting from immature to adult plumage, is fairly persistent.

Pictorella Finch (hen).
Although this Australian mannikin is easily sexed, the Pictorella is not a very popular species with aviculturists. This is due, no doubt, to its lack of bright colors, and the difficulties experienced when attempting to breed from it.

Pictorella Finch (cock).
This species spends a considerable amount of time on the floor of the aviary or cage. Because of this, caged birds would need to have the floor cleaned regularly, otherwise they could develop foot complaints.
In areas where damp, cold winters are experienced, the Pictorella should either be housed in roomy cages in a warm birdroom, or in indoor flights where the temperature can be easily controlled.

live food is not offered.

The most universal live food used is the mealworm. It is the larvae of the Flower Beetle, (*Tenebrio molitor*). It is bred in vast numbers commercially, and, unless you have a very large collection of birds which constantly require live food, it is probably easier to purchase mealworms as and when required, rather than to attempt to breed them yourself.

If kept for any length of time, the larvae will require feeding. Upon purchase, the mealworms should be placed in a clean container (a large biscuit tin with holes drilled into the lid, or an aquarium would prove suitable) with a quantity of bran (which they will eat). As a moisture source, small quantities of sliced apple can be placed on top of the bran. Whatever type of container is used, it must be covered, as if any of the

Mealworms are a readily available form of live food.

larvae eventually pupate, the resulting beetles will be able to fly and may escape into the birdroom.

The main disadvantage with mealworms is their tough outer skin, which many finches find difficult to penetrate. This can be overcome by nipping off the heads of the mealworms before feeding them to the birds. Mealworms slough their skins from time to time and at such times become whitish in color. At this stage of their development they are easily

tackled by even the smallest of finches and, when available, can be fed directly to your birds.

I have found that certain species (the Chestnut-breasted Finch especially) favor the actual pupae rather than the mealworm, and the breeding pairs I own are fed exclusively on these. If your birds will take the pupae, it can save a lot of effort. Another problem with feeding live mealworms (which have not had their heads removed), is that if the birds do not eat them almost immediately, the mealworms may escape from the feeding bowl into the birdroom or aviary.

Another form of live food which is relished by many Australian finches, is live ants' eggs. I emphasize 'live' as the dried eggs found in shops devoted to aquarium fish requisites are of no use whatsoever as bird food. Few aviculturists have the opportunity to collect ants' eggs directly from the wild, however these eggs are obtainable frozen and a quantity can be purchased and placed in a deep freeze. Small portions can be taken out daily, thawed out, and then fed to the birds.

Different species of wax-moth larvae have become available in recent years and all can be purchased from a supplier dealing in live foods. The soft-skinned larvae are much relished by certain species and it is well worth offering them to your finches.

Maggots, or gentles as they are often called, are a further source of live food. However, great care should be taken when feeding them to any form of livestock, as if the maggots are not completely clean (i.e., have food still in their gut), they can cause disease or even death in the animal to which they have been fed. Personally, I would not entertain using maggots under any circumstances.

If you do decide to offer maggots to your birds, then the maggots should be kept in an open-top container in clean bran for three or four days so that they can clean themselves, both internally and externally. Once all signs of food have disappeared from their gut (undigested food appears as a dark line or spot in the gut), the maggots can be fed to your birds.

All the above-mentioned live foods are bred commercially and can be purchased either from pet stores or, in cases of difficulty, directly from the breeders themselves. The majority of commercial breeders advertise regularly in cagebird magazines or journals.

It is also possible to collect certain live foods directly from the wild. At least one species of Australian finch (see CRIMSON FINCH), when rearing chicks, is keen to take any spiders offered. These can be taken from the wild either by collecting them individually by hand or by sweeping bushes, nettle beds, and such with a large fine-gauze net. Another method is to place an opened umbrella underneath a bush, shake the bush, and then close the umbrella, thus trapping any spiders or other invertebrates which have fallen into it. Upon arriving home, the umbrella can be taken into the aviary, opened up, and the contents released.

It would prove difficult to offer wild live food to caged birds, as even if you were able to place such food in the birds' cages, the majority of spiders and other small invertebrates would no doubt escape into the birdroom before the birds had the opportunity to catch and eat them. Because of this, it would be preferable to offer caged birds a type of live food over which a certain amount of control can be maintained.

LONG-TAILED GRASSFINCH
(*Poephila acuticauda*) (color photos on page 82)
Two subspecies of the Long-tailed Grassfinch are recognized: *P. a. acuticauda*, which has a yellow beak, and *P. a. hecki*, which has a red beak. The latter is known as the Heck's Grassfinch and so popular is it in aviculture that I have given it its own heading (see HECK'S GRASSFINCH), and so will discuss only the nominate race here.

Due to its long tail wires, the overall length of the Long-tailed Grassfinch is approximately 170 mm (6¾ in). However, approximately 38 mm of this are taken up by the twin tail wires. The crown and nape are gray; the mantle pinkish-fawn, with the back and wings brown. The upper-tail coverts are white, with a black band across the rump. The tail feathers are black, as are the lores, chin, throat, and upper breast. The remainder of the underparts are pinkish-fawn, except for the center of the lower abdomen and under-tail coverts, which are white. There is a large patch of black feathers on each flank. The beak is yellow.

Distribution is from the Kimberley region in Western Australia, across the top of the Northern Territory to the Gulf of Carpentaria, and east to the Leichardt river. The yellow-beaked nominate form is found throughout the western part of its range and the red-beaked race is found in the northern portion. The preferred habitat is mainly savannah grassland in sparsely timbered eucalypt woodland.

It appears that in Australia the Long-tail is common in aviculture, with the Heck's being considered rare. The Long-tail is also well established in the United States, where it is usually given the name Shaft-tail. In Europe it is the Heck's which is more commonly seen, due mainly to breeders preferring the deep red beak of the Heck's as compared to the yellow of the Long-tail. In the United Kingdom, Heck's are bred in vast numbers, whereas the Long-tail is in danger of being lost to aviculture (in its pure form, at any rate).

The Long-tail is recessive to the Heck's and if mated together all the resulting young will have reddish beaks. Due to in-discriminate mating over the years, *pure* Long-tails with deep yellow beaks are difficult to find in the United Kingdom. A good Long-tail should have a beak as yellow as that of the Masked Grassfinch, *P. personata*, and to maintain this coloring, only birds with well-colored beaks should be mated together. On no account should Long-tails be mated to the red-beaked Heck's, as, even when resulting young are mated back to yellow-beaked birds, it could be generations before birds with deep yellow beaks are produced.

As already mentioned, the progeny from a Heck's to a Long-tail mating (if the Heck's are pure) will have reddish beaks. They will, of course, be split for yellow, but so dominant is the red beak of the Heck's that even if split birds are mated to Long-tails, the

A Long-tailed Grassfinch at 13 days of age.

resulting young will still have a suffusion of red in the beak. There are presently many 'mongrel' birds around (in the United Kingdom), and these have neither the brilliant sealing-wax-red beak of the Heck's, nor the deep yellow beak of the Long-tail, but have either pale red or yellowish-pink beaks. If used for breeding, such birds should be mated to Heck's with well-colored beaks, but never to Long-tails.

It is unfortunate that the Long-tail is at present so rare in the United Kingdom. The species is easily bred, either in aviary accommodation or in a cage. They are extremely hardy birds and can remain in an aviary all the year round if a heated shelter is provided. They are suitable for a mixed collection, but only the larger, more robust Australian finches should be housed with them, as cock Long-tails in full breeding condition may bully other birds with which they are housed, especially if such birds are of a smaller, more timid species. On no account should they be housed with Masked, or Black-throated (Parson) Finches, as interbreeding may take place, and, for the reasons mentioned above, the Long-tail should never be housed with Heck's.

The usual clutch ranges from four to six eggs; incubation does not commence until the final egg is laid, although one or both of the pair may spend a considerable amount of time in the nest before incubation begins, and both birds will almost certainly sleep in the box. Incubation takes from 12 to 14 days. When the chicks are nine days of age, brooding ceases, although the hen (and sometimes the cock also) usually covers the chicks at night. The chicks can be closed-banded at approximately 12 days of age. They leave the nest at 21 days and can be removed from their parents between five and six weeks of age, as by then they will almost certainly be feeding themselves.

Most breeding pairs will take large quantities of soaked seeds, and many will also take a good proprietary brand of egg-food. Some pairs will also take green food, but I have never been able to persuade pairs, even with chicks, to take live food in any form.

Immature Long-tails resemble adults except that their plumage is duller, the black bib is much smaller, and the beak and legs are black. They begin to molt into adult plumage when they are approximately eight weeks of age, and by the time they are four months old the majority should have completed this molt. It should be emphasized that although they are in adult plumage, they will not be fully mature until they are at least nine months old.

Young cock birds begin to sing from around eight weeks of age and continue to do so regularly until they are approximately four months old. If, during this period, the birds are studied regularly, it should prove easy to pick out the cocks. Any which have not been seen to sing will almost certainly prove to be hens. If compared to known cock birds, the visual differences should then prove easier to detect.

A person who has had wide experience of both Long-tails and Heck's could, no doubt, sex fully adult birds by visual means. The cock has a much bolder appearance than the hen, with a rounder, more brightly colored head, and the black bib is larger and broader, with the black bar across the flanks being more pronounced. However, even the most experienced breeder can find the sex of certain individuals difficult to determine and the only sure way is by the song of the cock.

Although fully adult cocks may not sing as regularly as young birds, especially if housed with others of their kind, it is usually fairly simple to persuade an adult cock to sing by placing it in a cage on its own for a while (see SEXING).

Mutations of the Long-tail are reported as having been bred in Australia and the USA. It is doubtful if those reported in the UK are actual Long-tails; all the mutations I have seen have almost certainly been Heck's.

M

MASKED GRASSFINCH (*Poephila personata*) (color photos on page 82)

The overall length is approximately 130–140 mm (5–5½ in). From the forehead to the upper rump is cinnamon-brown, as are the wings. The lower rump and upper-tail coverts are white. The tail, sides of the forehead, lores, and edging to beak and chin are black. The throat and breast are cinnamon (paler than the upperparts); the abdomen and under-tail coverts are white with a black patch on each of the flanks. The beak is bright yellow.

The species is found in northern Australia, from Kimberley in Western Australia, across the Top End to Cape York Peninsula in Queensland. It favors sparsely wooded savannah and open grassland, near permanent water. Due to the human provision of stock-watering troughs, the species has been able to extend its range into otherwise dry areas.

Two subspecies are recognized. *P. p. personata* is found in the western and northern part of its range, east to the Leichardt river near the Gulf of Carpentaria. See WHITE-EARED GRASSFINCH for details of the other subspecies.

Probably the first thing one notices about the Masked Grassfinch is its brilliant yellow beak. It is not a particularly popular species, due, no doubt, to the difficulty one finds in locating true pairs. It has also proved difficult to breed. For those who wish to keep and attempt to breed the Masked, I would suggest that aviary accommodation would perhaps prove more suitable than a cage. If housed in the former, a heated shelter would have to be provided, and during the colder months of the year it would be prudent to bring the birds into a warm birdroom and cage them until weather conditions again permitted them to be released into an aviary.

As the Masked can prove very difficult to breed, it would be beneficial to offer both natural nesting sites (in the aviary flight) and nest boxes in the shelter. In the wild, the Masked usually builds its nest close to the ground; this should be allowed for when attempting aviary breeding by placing large tussocks of grass on the floor of the flight. Low bushes and creepers should also be made available.

The average clutch is between four and six eggs. Incubation takes approximately 13 to 15 days. The young usually fledge between 20 and 23 days and by the time they are five or six weeks of age they should be fully independent. Immature birds are dull brown with the facial mask gray; the beak and legs are black. They begin to molt into adult plumage fairly early in life, and by the time they are nine weeks of age they should be almost indistinguishable from adults. Needless to say, although at this early age they may have the appearance of an adult, they most certainly should not be used for breeding as they will not be fully developed until they are at least nine months of age.

Due to the difficulties experienced when attempting to breed the Masked, it would be prudent to give a pair, or a small colony, an aviary to themselves. If you do decide to house them in a mixed collection, then such species as Long-tails, Heck's, and Black-throated (Parson) should not be included, otherwise interbreeding may take place.

For someone who is keen to breed the Masked, but does not have aviary accommodation, then by all means house individual pairs in roomy box cages. They can be persuaded to breed under such conditions and a dedicated Australian finch enthusiast will, no doubt, if he or she perseveres, eventually succeed!

Of all the monomorphic Australian finches, the Masked is probably the most difficult to sex visually. The cocks supposedly have a brighter body color than the hens, and the face mask and the black flank bars are also more prominent and extensive in the cocks. However, unless a potential breeder can obtain guaranteed true pairs, it would be prudent to purchase at least half a dozen birds in the hope that one or two true pairs are among them. At first the birds could be housed together in an indoor flight or large cage, thus allowing them to choose their partners naturally. Once the birds have paired up, the true pairs could be moved to their breeding quarters.

MINERAL BLOCKS
One source of minerals which Australian finches without exception appear to enjoy, is 'cattle lick.' This is a mineral block which is, as the name implies, supplied for feeding to cattle. It can usually be purchased from suppliers of cattle feeds; alternatively, it may prove possible to obtain the small amount one would normally require from a farmer, especially if the latter owned a farm shop. Indeed, this is where I always obtain the supplies I need.

Cattle lick is usually sold in a large block (offered whole to cattle to enable them to lick it whenever they wish). Usually, when I require a fresh supply, I ask fellow aviculturists if they also need some and, if they do, we share the costs. The mineral block can, if dry, be easily sawn into small portions (approximately 5 cm/2 in square by 2.5 cm/1 in deep) which should then be placed on the cage floor, near to where the bath is normally situated. For aviary or flight birds, the portion could be a little larger; again, it should be placed near to a bath. The reason for this is that it is only when the block becomes moist that the birds find it attractive. If it is not possible to place the mineral block where it will remain moist, then every day or so it should be held under a running tap for a few moments, after which it can again be placed in the birds' quarters.

When the mineral blocks are moist, most species will spend a considerable time pecking (in certain cases actually licking) the blocks.

Occasionally the blocks will become soiled with droppings. If they do, then they should immediately be scrubbed under a running cold-water tap and placed back in position. In the United States, mineral blocks are available which are made specially for pet birds. (See also CHARCOAL GRANULES, GRIT.)

MITES

There are two species of mite to which Australian finches may fall prey: red mite (*Dessmanyssus gallinae*) and air-sac mite (*Stemostoma tracheacolum*).

The former is a fairly common parasite of cage birds. It is an agile, gray or brownish, long-legged mite which distends its body and turns bright red after feeding on the blood of its host. Usually the attack takes place during the night; during daylight hours the mite hides away in crevices.

As these mites feed on the birds' blood during the night, the birds often become listless, due no doubt to lack of proper rest and anemia. If the infestation is not checked, the birds will rapidly lose condition. If nest boxes become infested, breeding birds may desert their eggs or young.

Red mite can easily be eradicated by hanging a pest strip of the type normally used for killing houseflies in the infested cage, or, in the case of an aviary shelter, in the shelter itself. Many bird keepers hang a piece of this strip permanently in the birdroom or shelter. Such a practice has no ill effects on the birds and keeps their quarters free from all mite infestations.

The air-sac mite attacks the respiratory tract, causing coughing, sneezing, and loss of voice. Unless treatment is carried out, the infested bird will quickly lose condition and eventually die. As with red mite, a pest strip hung in the cage will quickly rid the bird, or birds, of such mites, and if the strip is left permanently in the birds' quarters, it will keep stock clear of such infestations.

At one time infestations of air-sac mite were prevalent among Gouldian Finches, especially when wild-caught birds were still being imported. Nowadays it is rare to hear of a case. However, the wild Gouldian is declining rapidly in numbers and some researchers blame the decline on the fact that so many wild birds are infested with air-sac mite.

Aviary birds infested with air-sac mite would need to be caught up and caged in a birdroom, when the above treatment could then be carried out. Once free from the infestation, they could be released into the aviary again.

If an aviary became infested with red mite, then, as mentioned earlier, a pest strip could be hung in the shelter. However, if the infestation proved difficult to eradicate, it would be prudent to remove the birds to other quarters and thoroughly clean the aviary, preferably with a dilution of disinfectant, and then spray all walls and perches with an antimite solution, after which the birds could be released back into the aviary.

Unlike red mite, feather mites (of which there are a number of species), actually live on their hosts. The infestation begins with the mites feeding on their hosts' feathers and their presence can usually be detected by inspecting the birds' flight and tail feathers. If small patches of the feathers appear to have been eaten away around the central spine, then it is almost certain that mites are present. If left unchecked, the mites will, as they continue to breed, eventually infest the central quills of developing feathers and the birds' plumage will be destroyed.

As with red and air-sac mites, feather mites can be eliminated by placing a pest strip in the infested birds' quarters. Various preparations are also available for the treatment of all these mites, either in an aerosol spray or as a powder. Insecticides containing pyrethrin (a natural substance that is harmless to birds) are also effective. The insecticide Cabaryl is another useful one to choose. Such preparations should be administered exactly as prescribed by the manufacturer.

It should be explained that the pest strip should only be hung in a *cage* where there is a mite infestation and even then the strip must be covered with gauze to prevent the birds from reaching it. Once the infestation has been eradicated, the strip should be removed from the cage, but one can be left permanently in the birdroom or aviary shelter to prevent a further outbreak.

MOLT

The molt from immature to adult plumage can prove to be a critical period with certain species of Australian finch, and extra care is required at such times. As all my

MONOMORPHIC SPECIES, A GUIDE TO VISUAL SEXING

Species	Distinguishing features between adult birds cock (♂) and hen (♀)
Beautiful Firetail	Center of abdomen, ♂ black, ♀ lacks patch, has more barring.
Bicheno Finch	Face mask, ♂ silvery-white, ♀ off-white. Breast, ♂ silvery-white, ♀ grayish-white.
Black-throated Finch	As for Long-tailed Grassfinch, also head of ♂ silver-gray, ♀ sooty-gray (except for Black-rumped form).
Blue-faced Parrot Finch	Body color, ♂ grass-green, ♀ slightly duller. Face, ♂ cobalt-blue, extending back over forehead and around eyes, ♀ duller blue and less extensive.
Chestnut-breasted Finch	Crown and nape, ♂ silver-blue, ♀ gray. Breast, ♂ deep chestnut, ♀ paler.
Diamond Firetail	Head color, ♂ silver-gray, ♀ darker gray. Beak color (in breeding condition), ♂ maroon, ♀ coral-pink.
Long-tailed Grassfinch	Black throat-patch, ♂ wider and deeper than in ♀. Flank bars, ♂ wider and more prominent that in ♀. Head, ♂ more rounded and bolder than in ♀.
Masked Grassfinch	Overall color, ♂ brighter than ♀. Black mask and bar across flanks, ♂ more prominent and extensive than in ♀.
Red-browed Finch	Eye stripe, ♂ extends further behind eye and is square at end, ♀ stripe shorter and tapers at end.
Red-eared Firetail	During nonbreeding season, sexes almost identical. In breeding condition, ♂ ear coverts deep scarlet, ♀ more orange.
Yellow-rumped Finch	Head color, ♂ silvery-gray, ♀ darker gray.

breeding pairs are supplied with freely available soaked seeds for the whole of the breeding season, young birds receive these seeds from birth. As I believe soaked seeds are extremely beneficial, I continue to supply these seeds to young birds until they have completed the molt into full adult plumage, after which the supply is discontinued until the birds are actually put down to breed.

The Gouldian Finch is notorious for the length of time it can take certain youngsters to adopt full adult plumage, and many breeders have, in the past, reported losses of up to half their young birds during this critical period. Nowadays fewer young appear to be lost during the molt, no doubt due to the Gouldian Finch having become virtually domesticated and, because of this, more used to captive conditions. Many young Gouldians often complete their first molt in a period of four months, but some can take almost a year and periods of 18 months have been recorded. Some young birds may not even attain full adult plumage until their second year! If such birds have only a small number of immature feathers remaining, I see nothing wrong in using them for breeding. Birds that have only a small

An immature Gouldian Finch. Note how tame some of these birds can become.

amount of adult plumage, however (even if they are a year or more of age) should not, in my opinion, be used for breeding, since there is every possibility they will pass on to their offspring the inability to molt out correctly.

Certain other species, such as Bichenos, Chestnut-breasted, Long-tails, and Plum-headed, molt into adult plumage early in life. Bichenos, for instance, can be in full adult plumage within ten weeks of hatching. Star Finches also begin to molt at an early age. However, this species has a sub-adult plumage before it finally molts into full adult dress and therefore Stars cannot be classed as fully adult until at least nine months of age.

Once the first molt is completed, no further difficulties should be experienced, as the annual process of replenishing feathers usually proceeds without problems in adult Australian finches.

During the annual molt, some adult birds (especially Gouldians) may be seen to sit around with their heads tucked over their backs. Usually this is not a cause for concern, but should this persist, it would be prudent to raise the temperature of the birdroom a little.

MONOMORPHIC SPECIES
The table on the opposite page is meant only as a guide. It is extremely difficult to sex mono-morphic Australian finches by visual means and the only truly reliable method is by the song of the cock bird.

With regard to the Heck's Grassfinch, the same features apply as described for the Long-tail.

N

NEST BOXES

If in full breeding condition, Australian finches will attempt to nest in almost any receptacle. Nevertheless, it is preferable to supply a standard nest box. If you keep a variety of species, especially as a mixed collection in an aviary or indoor flight, offering identical nest boxes will help to discourage bickering among breeding birds. If all your stock is housed in cages, the use of identical nest boxes would mean that all cage layouts could be the same and a cage can then be used for whatever species you keep at the time, without having to move fittings around to accommodate a different type of nest box.

I have found a 13 cm (5 in) cubed, all-wood nest box to be ideal. The front opening should be no more than 4 cm (1½ in). This means that the front panel needs to be approximately 8 cm (3 in) in height. Such a height ensures that, after the nest has been completed, an incubating bird can be completely hidden from view. Should the bird wish to look out of the box, it has only to stand up to do so. A hinged lid should be fitted to the nest box, thus allowing easy access to the nest.

A nest box as used by the author. Note the hinged lid which allows easy access to the nest — essential if you wish to fit chicks with closed-bands.

Many breeders hang the nest box on the wire front of the cage, with the opening facing inward. I always hang the nest box in a rear corner of the cage, allowing approximately 10 cm (4 in) between the top of the box and the roof of the cage, with the opening facing into the center of the cage. Placing a nest box in this way means that when someone enters the birdroom, an incubating bird has only to look out to see what is happening. Once assured that all is well, the bird can then settle back on the nest. With the nest box facing inward, an incubating bird would need to vacate the nest.

The reason I allow approximately 10 cm (4 in) between the top of the nest box and the roof of the cage is that many cock birds like to sit 'on guard' on the top of the box (Gouldians especially) while the hen is inside.

In aviaries, nest boxes should be placed as high as possible in the shelter. More boxes should be supplied than there are breeding pairs, thus allowing the birds to choose a box with a minimum of bickering. This also applies to birds kept on the colony system in an indoor flight.

When cage-breeding Gouldian Finches, I always remove the nest box when the chicks are approximately one month old, otherwise the parent birds may go to nest before the young are

Breeding pairs will sometimes refuse to enter the nest box, attempting instead to nest on top of the box. If an L-shaped piece of wood is placed on the top of the nest box, thus preventing the birds from sitting there, they will enter the nest box more readily. Once they have done so, the piece of wood can be removed.

weaned. It is possible for a breeding pair to go down to nest successfully while the young of the previous nest are still housed with them, but, more often than not, the eggs prove infertile, or become chipped or broken because of the young roosting in the nest box. The moment the young are removed, the cage should be given a thorough cleaning and the nest box again placed in position. If the pair are left too long without the nest box, they may go into a molt.

I must emphasize that it is only with Gouldian Finches that I remove the nest box *before* the chicks are weaned. Other species, even those breeding in cages, are allowed to keep their nest box until the chicks are weaned. However, the moment the chicks are removed, the nest box (even if it contains eggs) is also removed, thoroughly cleaned, and fresh nesting material is added before placing it back in position. It is rare for a pair to refuse to accept the cleaned nest box. If they do, then any eggs already laid would have to be discarded. However, the birds should quickly go down to nest again, and within a week or so the hen should have begun to lay a further clutch. Some people may consider it somewhat drastic to take away a nest box which already contains eggs, but I would rather lose that round of eggs than allow a pair to rear a further clutch in a

box in which they have already reared one brood.

Immediately after the breeding season is over, nest boxes should be removed, thoroughly cleaned, washed in a dilution of disinfectant and hot water, and stored away ready for use the following season. Any which have become damaged should be refurbished. Certain boxes may have become too fouled to clean properly; these should be discarded.

NEST INSPECTION
To obtain the maximum breeding potential from your birds, regular inspection of the nest box is necessary, otherwise a pair could be left incubating infertile eggs. Also, chicks which have hatched but are not being fed correctly by their parents, could be lost if the nest box is not inspected.

An incubating or brooding bird should never be forced from the nest. Certain Australian finches, such as Stars, are notoriously light sitters, leaving the nest at the least provocation. Try to avoid this occurrence. One can usually find both birds away from the nest at some time during the day and, at such times, the contents of the nest box can be inspected.

Infertile eggs can usually be identified at a glance, as they appear paler in color than fertile eggs. Once a breeder becomes used to the appearance of infertile eggs,

Gouldian Finch chicks at nine days of age. Note their well-filled crops. It is essential to inspect nests to ensure that the parent birds are feeding their chicks correctly.

there is little need to remove the whole clutch for inspection. Although infertile eggs can be identified approximately five days after incubation has begun, it is preferable to leave well enough alone until a week has elapsed before testing the eggs for fertility. If the whole clutch proves infertile, remove it, and in a matter of days the birds should go down to nest again.

If only one or two eggs prove fertile, these could be removed and either given to another pair who have been incubating for approximately the same length of time, but who also have only one or two fertile eggs, or fostered out to Society Finches. However, if a pair are to be allowed to incubate and raise chicks from only two eggs, then the whole of the clutch must be left with them. To remove all but the two fertile eggs would almost certainly cause the pair to desert. It is unlikely that a pair will successfully rear a solitary chick, as with so little to occupy him, the cock may attempt to drive the hen to nest again before the chick is reared. Therefore, if only one chick hatches from a clutch, it is best fostered out to another pair of the same species or to Societys with a chick or chicks of a similar age.

NEST SITES IN THE WILD

The selection of nest sites is influenced by the habitat in which the bird lives. Most Australian finches tend to breed in bushes or small trees. The Painted Firetail, however, nests in spinifex grass, near to the ground. The Pictorella, Plum-headed, Chestnut-breasted, and Yellow-rumped prefer to nest in reeds or tall grasses. The Red-eared Firetail usually builds its nest high up in tall eucalypts.

The Gouldian Finch has almost completely switched to hole-nesting, usually nesting in a small hollow in a tree or termite mound. Inside the hollow, the birds build a small nest with thin walls and without any entrance tunnel; many nests even lack a roof. In some breeding pairs the nest-building drive appears to have disappeared almost completely, and nests have been found at the bottom of a hollow, with little or no nesting material at all added.

The above is borne out from experience with captive birds. Few Gouldian Finch pairs attempt to construct a nest in the box provided, and unless nesting material is added to the nest box *before* being placed in the bird's quarters, few pairs show any interest in nesting. (See GOULDIAN FINCH.)

All Australian finches attempt to protect their nests from predators, using a variety of methods: some hang the nests on twigs above water, others favor the vicinity of wasps' nests, and some species build in thorny trees. Bicheno Finches have been recorded nesting near to comb-nests of stinging wasps.

Most Australian finches construct domed nests with a side entrance and an entrance tunnel. The nests of species which build in the tops of trees or between grass stems are characterized by their great strength. Those species which inhabit semideserts, on the other hand, are limited by the availability of nesting material, and often construct very flimsy nests.

In many cases the nest has a strong outer layer, while the inner part is softer and more substantial. The length of the pieces of nest material decreases toward the center. In the main, green or dried grass stems are used for nest building, the percentage varying according to the species. Many species line the nest with soft material, white feathers being preferred for this purpose.

NESTING MATERIAL

It has been mentioned earlier (see NEST BOXES) that Australian finches housed in aviaries should be supplied with nest boxes. However, should the aviary be planted out with shrubs, it is possible that certain species will build in these and, quite likely, successfully hatch and rear their young in a nest made entirely by the breeding pair. Aviary birds should therefore be supplied with sufficient nesting material with which to build a nest should they so desire. Soft hay should be hung around the aviary in loosely tied bundles, within easy access of the birds.

Certain species will build their nest in the nest boxes provided whether they are housed in cages, aviaries, or indoor flights. However, it is preferable to fill the nest boxes with good-quality soft

Gouldian Finch chicks at one day old (and one egg). Note the type of hay used by Gouldian Finches for nest-building.

hay before placing them in position, as most species, especially when housed in cages, prefer to take over an already filled box, only added a small amount of material themselves.

Some breeders supply coconut fiber as nesting material. I have used this in the past, but found that with certain species the nest was inclined to 'sweat.' Nowadays I use soft hay or, in certain cases, a mixture of soft hay and coconut fiber, but never the latter on its own.

Before placing nesting material in the nest box, it is advisable to add a layer of clean white sawdust (about 25 mm/1 in deep). This not only helps to keep the nest dry, it will also make it easier for you to remove the soiled nesting material after the birds have raised chicks.

After filling the nest box with hay, one's balled fist should be forced into the hay, thus forming a nest hollow. If coconut fiber alone is used, then an almost perfect nest hollow can be formed.

Gouldian Finches appear to move around in the nest when incubating, and because of this it is essential that fresh pieces of hay, approximately 23 cm (9 in) in length, are used to fill the box, as shorter, more brittle pieces may, due to the continual movement of the birds, eventually cover the eggs and the birds will then desert.

Even though I have

recommended that nest boxes be filled with hay, it is important to offer a small amount of nesting material outside of the box so that the birds can, if they wish, add to the nest. For aviary birds and those housed in indoor flights, the material can, as already mentioned, be hung in loose bundles within easy access of the birds. For caged birds, a small amount should be placed on the cage floor. Directly under the nest box is an ideal place as it should not then become soiled with droppings.

Certain individuals (usually the cock birds) may continue to add to the nest well after incubation has commenced, and because of this eggs could inadvertently become covered, causing the pair to desert. It is advisable, therefore, to remove all nesting material from the cage once incubation has begun. One exception to this is the Star Finch, as, in my experience, cock birds of this species appear to become bored when the hen is incubating. Unless a certain amount of material is left in the cage, cock Stars will (probably for want of something else to do) begin to remove hay from the nest. Such behavior could eventually almost denude the nest, thus causing the hen to desert.

Certain species of Australian finch, such as Stars, Bichenos, and Diamond Firetails, use pieces of hay for display purposes. I have always found that the material used for display is unlike that which would be used for nest building, in that it is always long, stiff pieces which are selected, rather than those that are more soft and pliable. Because of this, it would be prudent to offer such species two or three long, coarse pieces of hay to enable the cock birds (and in the case of Stars, the hens also) to use these when they wish to display to their mates (see COURTSHIP DISPLAY).

NESTS, ROOSTING
Nine species of Australian finch are reported to build a 'nest' which is used for roosting purposes only. Under caged conditions it would prove virtually impossible for breeding pairs to construct a nest solely for roosting; indeed, under these conditions few species will even attempt to build a nest at all, preferring to accept a nest box already filled with hay (see NEST BOXES and NESTING MATERIAL). However, when housed in a planted aviary and allowed to build their own nests in the shrubs or bushes growing in the flight, it is possible that certain breeding pairs will, as well as building a breeding nest, also build a nest for roosting. The latter is usually a smaller structure than the breeding nest, does not have an entrance tunnel, and remains unlined.

Species which have been known to construct roosting nests are: Diamond Firetail, Beautiful Firetail, Red-eared Firetail, Red-browed Finch, Bicheno Finch, Masked Grassfinch, Long-tailed Grassfinch, Black-throated (or Parson) Finch, and Zebra Finch.

OUTBREEDING
The term outbreeding describes the continual pairing of birds from unrelated stock. Obviously, someone taking up the breeding of a species for the first time has to purchase birds bred by others and, for the first season at least, has to outbreed with the birds. However, if you decide to keep (and maybe breed) a species that is new to you, it would, if at all possible, be beneficial to purchase the breeding pair (or pairs) from one source. If you are able to do this, then at the time of purchase, ask to see the parents of the birds you are buying. You will then have an idea as to what the youngsters produced from the birds you are purchasing will be like.

If you purchase birds indiscriminately from different sources, then you will have no idea what the youngsters from such birds will be like, as although the birds you have purchased may appear to be of good quality, when they produce young, hidden traits which are not apparent in the adults may be reproduced in their offspring.

Selective outbreeding can prove useful in maintaining or improving the quality of inbred or linebred birds. For example, if a particular trait in a given strain has been weakened through several generations of line- or inbreeding, then outcrossing with an unrelated bird which excels in the trait you wish to strengthen may assist in restoring the weakened trait. It is important, however, that the outcross is not deficient in any of the good points which have already been established in the inbred or linebred strain.

To give an example: If you have been inbreeding or linebreeding for a number of generations, and you feel that the young produced are excellent in everything except size, then you may decide to purchase a bird (as an outcross) which excels in size, so that this trait can be introduced into your own birds. If your birds, although lacking in size, are of excellent color and markings, then the outcross you decide to purchase must, as well as being of good size, be of excellent color and markings also, otherwise the outcross may put size into your stud, but will also introduce poor color and markings.

It must always be remembered that indiscriminate or nonselective outcrossing can easily destroy the many years of work you have put into establishing a good strain of quality inbred or linebred birds.

OWL FINCH (see BICHENO FINCH)

PAINTED FINCH (see PAINTED FIRETAIL)

PAINTED FIRETAIL (*Emblema picta*) (color photos on pages 54–55) The Painted Firetail is, without doubt, one of the most beautiful of all the Australian finches. The cocks have upperparts of pale brown, except for the rump and upper-tail coverts which are scarlet, as are the lores, forehead, forepart of the cheeks, the chin, and the upper throat. The tail feathers are dusky-brown. The foreneck, breast, and abdomen are black, spotted with white, with an irregular line of scarlet down the center of the breast. The under-tail coverts are black. The beak is black, tipped with red on the upper mandible; the lower mandible is red with a blue base. The total length is approximately 110–114 mm (4⅓–4½ in).

Hens differ slightly from cock birds in that only the lores and the feathers above the eyes and at the base of the lower mandible are scarlet. The underparts are duller black, with larger white spots and with less scarlet on the breast.

The Painted Firetail is found from the Kimberley and Pilbara regions of north Western Australia, through the Northern Territory, east to the Rolling Downs region in Queensland, and south to the Musgrave and Everard ranges in northern South Australia. It inhabits dry, arid areas, but is usually found close to permanent water along gorges, rocky hills, and stony ridges covered with spinifex.

The species is often referred to as the Painted Finch. In aviculture it is extremely scarce except in Australia where, it appears, the species is classed as 'common.' In the United States and the United Kingdom, numbers are very low and, due to close-breeding, the majority lack vigor, so that few pairs even attempt to breed.

So popular is the species in its country of origin that it is recommended as being ideal for the beginner, due to being

A Painted Firetail at one day old, plus three fertile eggs. Note the mouth markings.

inexpensive, docile, and easy to breed!

Being dimorphic, the Painted is readily sexed. From all accounts it is easy to persuade a pair to nest in either a cage (which must be fairly large) or aviary, and one therefore wonders why numbers are so low outside of Australian aviculture.

The Painted is a fairly hardy species and can be housed in aviary accommodation as long as an adequately heated shelter is provided. However, due to its great rarity, anyone fortunate enough to own a pair (outside of Australia) would no doubt prefer to house them in a large cage in a birdroom. The species can be persuaded to take to a con-ventional nest box, but most prefer to build their own nests, either close to, or on the floor of, their cage or flight. Some can be persuaded to take to a canary wicker nest basket, especially if it is attached to a firm base and partly camouflaged with small twigs or stems of coarse grass.

The average clutch size is four eggs. Incubation does not commence until the final egg of the clutch is laid, and hatching takes

place 13 to 14 days later. The young birds leave the nest when they are between 23 and 26 days old, at first spending a considerable amount of time on the floor, usually huddled together in a corner.

Immature birds are basically a dull brown color; the beak is black. The molt from immature to adult plumage is usually completed by the time the birds are 16 weeks of age. Young cocks can usually be picked out soon after the molt from immature to adult plumage begins, by the red feathers which appear on the breast.

Live food can be offered to adult pairs with young. They may also be persuaded to take a certain amount of soft food at such times.

A 'yellow' mutation is being bred successfully in Australia, in which the scarlet on the face, rump, and abdomen of the male is replaced by rusty orange-yellow.

PAIRING UP
Birds should be in full breeding condition before being placed in their breeding quarters. If the sexes have been housed separately, the cock birds, when in condition, will

be seen to sing regularly, and many will continually call to the hens. If the floor of the cage is covered with newspaper, caged birds will often tear strips from the paper and carry these around. In the Gouldian Finch, the cock, when in condition, usually develops an almost white beak, with only the tip colored.

Many hens begin to lay eggs as soon as they are in breeding condition, even though they are segregated from the cock birds. Hens also show a prominent rise to the rump and may hold the tail in a downward position. Hen Gouldian Finches usually develop an almost black beak when ready for breeding.

Breeding pairs that are to be housed in cages should be introduced to their cage at the same time. Alternatively, a cock could be placed in the cage a few days before the hen, but never place a hen in the breeding cage before the cock bird, as it is likely, once used to the cage, that the hen would prove dominant over a newly introduced cock and, as he may never assert himself, mating might not take place. In this event, the pair would have to be split up for a while before they could again be placed together.

PARSON FINCH (see BLACK-THROATED FINCH)

PECTORELLA FINCH (see PICTORELLA FINCH)

PERCHES
More often than not, little thought is given to the type of perches supplied, yet when one remembers that a large part of a bird's life is spent on a perch, it should be obvious that serious consideration must be given to this most important item.

Birds housed in aviary accommodation will, if the outside flight is planted, have shrubs and bushes in which to perch, but, nevertheless, alternative perching should be supplied. The flight should not be so cluttered with perches that the birds find it difficult to exercise, but I would recommend that at least one or two perches be placed at each end of the flight, fairly high up. In the shelter, roosting perches would need to be placed fairly high up to encourage the birds to roost there.

A number of perches would also need to be fixed at lower positions, especially near to, but not directly above, the feeding station. All perches should be firmly fixed, as loose perches could affect fertility in those species which mate on a perch, if the copulating birds are unable to obtain a firm grip on the perch. I much prefer to use natural perches and one of the best is new growth taken from elder (*Sambucus nigra*) as it is usually not only straight, but is also soft and pliable.

Elder can be found in damp woods, hedges, and on waste land. If taken from woods or hedges, then permission may be needed. However, I have always been able to find enough growing on waste areas for my needs. No matter where the elder is taken from, it should always be thoroughly scrubbed before using it for perches. If you are unable to obtain new growth, then older branches can still be used, but I usually smooth these down slightly with fine-grade sandpaper.

Elder also makes suitable perching for inside flights (and cages – see below), and if cut in late spring, when the new growth has hardened slightly, it is ideal.

For caged birds, I find the twist-on perches usually supplied for canaries to be fine. These perches can be fitted to the cage front in any position required. As they are only attached to the wire front of the cage, each time a bird lands on them they move slightly. Because of this, they are far superior to perches which are fixed to the cage front and the rear wall, as the latter do not move at all when birds alight on them and the hard landing can jar the birds somewhat as they move from perch to perch. Also, the use of fixed perches, especially if made of hard wood, can, over a period, cause the birds to develop foot problems.

Another point in favor of twist-on perches is that they are easily removed for cleaning purposes. If a number of spares are kept, a soiled perch can be replaced with a clean one in seconds. If twist-on perches are used, they should be made of softwood and be no more than 9 mm (3/8 in) thick. When I purchase a new batch of these perches, I always smooth down the edges with sandpaper, making them slightly more rounded, as I feel they are then more comfortable for the birds.

Natural perches can, of course, be used in cages and if these are preferred then I would again suggest elder be used. Lengths of this wood can be sawn into sections which are slightly longer than the depth of the cage. A groove can then be cut into one end (to fit onto the cage front) and either a small nail or half of a cocktail stick can be forced into the other end of the perch. If a small hole is then drilled into the back of the cage, the nail or cocktail stick can be forced into this hole and the perch will be held firmly in place. Some bird keepers fix perches in a cage by cutting the perch slightly longer than the cage is deep; the perch is then held in position by tension between the wire front and the back wall of the cage.

Under no circumstances would I use hardwood doweling for perches. Not only do such perches prove to be extremely hard on the birds' feet, but they do not allow a bird to obtain a proper grip and this could cause infertile eggs to be produced.

Natural perches need to be replaced regularly as eventually they become too brittle and hard for the birds' comfort. Although twist-on perches will last virtually forever, they should be interchanged with clean ones regularly. The soiled perches can then be soaked in a dilution of disinfectant and warm water, thoroughly scrubbed, and stored ready for immediate use.

PICTORELLA FINCH (*Lonchura pectoralis*) (color photos on page 95)

The vernacular name of this finch can be spelled with an 'i' or an 'e,' hence Pectorella Finch is the same species as Pictorella.

Its approximate total length is 101–110 mm (4–4⅓ in). The adult cock, from forehead to upper-tail coverts, is grayish-brown. The primaries are brown, paler on the outer webs. Upper-wing coverts are also brown with minute white dots at the tip. Tail feathers are dusky-brown; the lores black; the sides of the face, ear coverts, and throat are glossy purple-black. A fawn line extends from the sides of

the forehead over the eye to the sides of the neck, where it becomes broader and slightly brighter in color. The breast is white, each feather having a subterminal black bar. The remainder of the underparts is light vinaceous-drown. The beak is bluish-gray.

Adult hens are similar in plumage to the cock but the feathers on the sides of the face, ear coverts, and throat are brownish-black. Those of the breast have a somewhat broader subterminal black bar, giving the whole breast a black-and-white barred appearance.

The species is found in the drier parts of northern Australia, from Kimberley in the west to the Gulf of Carpentaria in the east. The preferred habitat is acacia scrubland, where there is a grassy undergrowth; the species is also found in dry spinifex country. The Pictorella is known to interbreed in the wild with the Chestnut-breasted Finch.

Although this Australian mannikin is easily sexed, the Pictorella is not a very popular species with aviculturists, due, no doubt, to its lack of bright colors and the difficulties experienced when attempting to breed from it.

Pictorellas spend a considerable amount of time on the floor of their aviary or cage, where their courtship display is also carried out. Because of this, caged birds would need to have the floor cleaned regularly, otherwise they could develop foot complaints. In aviaries the most natural setting would be for clumps of grass to be placed at strategic positions on the floor of the outside flight. The birds would then almost certainly use these as nesting sites.

If caged, Pictorellas will certainly use nest boxes, but under such conditions they prove extremely light sitters, leaving the nest at the least disturbance. Some enthusiasts have found that an open-topped nest box, placed in a rear corner of the cage, often persuades a pair to nest more successfully. However, it is difficult to persuade a pair actually to lay eggs, incubate, and successfully rear young under caged conditions.

Another problem is that although Societys willingly foster the young from Pictorella Finches, the success rate can prove

112

somewhat low. This may be because, unlike other Australian finch chicks which call for food, Pictorella chicks are virtually mute for the first week or so and the Societys do not respond to them.

Perhaps if fosters that have never reared young before were used, the success rate might be higher, as the Societys would not have had experience with the more vocal species and, because of this, would feed the almost mute Pictorellas as if rearing such chicks was the norm.

The average clutch size is five eggs. During the day, both birds take turns in incubating, but only the hen sits at night. Young birds which are almost fully feathered (at approximately 16 to 18 days of age) will leave the nest at the least provocation, and, in most cases, it proves almost impossible to persuade them to return. Therefore, at this period of growth care should be taken not to frighten the chicks in any way. Normally, the chicks will leave the nest at the age of three weeks, but even then they can prove extremely nervous and care should be taken not to stress them unduly.

Live food, in the form of mealworms or live ants' eggs, should be offered to adult pairs with chicks, but such food should be rationed, otherwise the cock bird may become overstimulated and abandon the chicks in favor of preparing another nest.

In areas where damp, cold winters are experienced, the Australian finch enthusiast who wishes to take up the breeding of Pictorellas is in something of a dilemma; should he or she wish to breed the species successfully then, by all accounts, aviary accommodation is the most suitable. However, as the species is susceptible to damp and cold, and as it spends a considerable amount of time on the aviary floor, it could prove difficult to provide the correct conditions. Perhaps the ideal way in which to house the species would be as individual pairs in small indoor flights where the temperature could easily be controlled and yet pseudonatural conditions could be supplied. Pictorella Finches can be bred successfully in cages, but, as already mentioned, under these conditions few keepers appear to be successful in persuading the birds to rear their young to independence.

There are no known mutations in the Pictorella Finch, which is not surprising considering the small numbers bred each year.

PLANTS FOR AVIARIES

The choice of plants will clearly be influenced by the prevailing weather conditions in the area in which you live. Much will also depend on the design of your aviary. If, as suggested earlier (see AVIARIES), you have decided to cover your aviary floor with either gravel or concrete, then the plants you choose must be suitable for containers. If, on the other hand, you intend to grow plants directly in the soil of the aviary floor, your choice will be almost unlimited.

The following is a representative sample of suitable plants. Those unsuitable for containers are marked with an asterisk.

Annual Hop (*Humulus japonicus*). This can be sown each year from seed. It makes rapid growth.

Bamboo (*Sinarudinaria* spp.)*. Clumps produce good cover for birds and would be appreciated by Australian mannikins. However, it will require regular trimming, otherwise it may become too tall for the average garden aviary.

Blackberry (*Rubus fruticosus*)*. This provides excellent cover and attracts insects. There are thornless varieties which would, no doubt, prove most suitable. It would need to be kept under control, otherwise it may eventually take over the aviary completely.

Canary Creeper (*Tropaeolum multiflorus*). Sow seeds in April or May and the plant will then twine itself up the aviary wire. It can grow 3 m (10 ft) or more in a season. It produces canary-yellow flowers. It is suitable for a container, so you could sow seeds directly into the container in which you wish them to grow. Two or three planted together are more suitable as they give a better display than a plant grown on its own.

Clematis (*Clematis* spp.). Certain

Crimson Finches

Crimson Finch (cock) – White-bellied race. Crimson Finches (in both forms) are rare in aviculture and because of this are some of the most expensive of all the Australian finches.

Crimson Finch (hen) – White-bellied race. As can be seen when comparing this photograph with the previous one, the Crimson Finch is easily sexed as the hen is paler on her upperparts than the cock, and the crimson is restricted to the face and throat, with the remainder of the underparts ashy, and with white spotting along the flanks.

Crimson Finch (cock) – Black-bellied race. In the past both forms have had a reputation for being aggressive, not only to their own kind, but to other birds with which they are housed. However, it is now thought that much of this supposed aggression is, in fact, part of the mating display and is therefore harmless. Nevertheless, if you intend to house a breeding pair of Crimson Finches with other species, strict observation should be maintained, especially during the breeding season. Obviously, the Crimson Finch is not suitable for the newcomer to Australian finches.

Parrot Finches

Blue-faced Parrot Finch (hen). Although difficult to sex by visual means, certain hens (such as the one depicted here) have less extensive blue on the facial area. Also, their overall body color is less intense than in the cocks.

Blue-faced Parrot Finch (cock). The Blue-faced is the only parrot finch found in Australia. It is a robust species and it is possible to house these birds in an aviary all year round as long as access to a heated shelter is available.

Blue-faced Parrot Finch – Lutino mutation.
This is the only mutation which has appeared so far in the Blue-faced. The overall color is yellow, although birds are to be found in varying shades from deep yellow to pale lemon. The face mask, and flight and tail feathers are white and the rump is red (paler than in the Normal bird). The beak is also white. It appears to be as robust and as easily bred as the Normal Blue-faced.

An outdoor aviary which is connected to an indoor flight. This is ideal for housing and breeding most Australian finch species. Note the use of plants outside the aviary, thus helping to break up the outline of the structure and giving the inmates a more secluded enviroment.

species (such as *montana*) will quickly cover the aviary. As all species, if cared for correctly, flower well during their season, they can make a most attractive aviary plant. All clematis like their roots to be shaded. Many are suitable as container plants.

Conifers (various species). Many of the dwarf conifers are ideal as container plants. Being evergreen, they are useful during the winter months when many other plants will either have lost their leaves or have died down. However, conifers are really of ornamental value only, as birds would find it difficult to perch (or nest) in all but the larger varieties. Also, should the conifers become soiled with bird droppings, you would find it extremely difficult to clean them. Conifers are probably best used either as ornamental plants outside the aviary (to help break up the outline of the flight) or as wind-breaks. Fast-growing varieties, such as 'Leylandi,' are ideal as windbreaks, with the smaller, slow-growing species being more suitable for ornamental purposes.

Dog Rose (*Rosa canina*)*. This requires pruning to keep it under control, otherwise it is an attractive plant which, when in flower, gives off a beautiful scent.

Grasses. Certain types of grasses can make ideal plants for the aviary. All can be grown either directly in the ground or in containers. Some form ideal ground cover (see PICTORELLA FINCH), and after flowering, when the seeds become ripe, they can prove an added attraction for the birds.

Hawthorn (or May) (*Crataegus monogyna*)*. When well grown, this shrub is ideal for nesting sites. It can grow fairly large and would need pruning regularly. It produces dense flowers in early spring, followed later by berries. It is deciduous.

Honeysuckle (*Lonicera* spp.). This is an evergreen, with vigorous growth and beautiful flowers during late spring and through the summer. It needs to be pruned regularly. It can be grown in a container, but would require good support and heavy pruning each year if it is not to become too unwieldy. Under such conditions, it would also require feeding during the growing and flowering period.

Mock Orange (*Philadelphus coronarius*)*. This common shrub is also sometimes called syringa. It has fragrant flowers during late spring and early summer and is ideal for nesting sites. It needs to be kept under control by regular pruning. It is deciduous.

Morning Glory (*Ipomaea* spp.). Also known as the annual convolvulus. Sow seeds directly into a container. It has large blue, white, or red trumpetlike flowers which close after noon.

Perennial Pea (*Lathyrus latifolius*). This will climb up wire and makes a suitable plant for the rear wall of a flight. It dies down each year. Flowers appear in July through August. It would be suitable for a container. If grown directly in the ground, this plant would need to be controlled, otherwise it could spread to all parts of the aviary. It is difficult to eradicate when no longer required (you have been warned!).

Russian Vine (*Abies alba*)*. Extremely vigorous, this climber can grow as much as 3 m (10 ft) per year and in all but a very large aviary it would probably require pruning regularly to keep it in check. Ideal if you want to add foliage to the aviary as quickly as possible.

Snowball Tree (*Viburnum opulus*). Large, round, white flowers like snowballs are borne in May and June and are followed by translucent, red, slightly ovoid berries in autumn. It is most attractive, but would need controlling by regular pruning. It is deciduous. It may be suitable for a container but this would have to be fairly large and the plant would require feeding during the growing and flowering period.

Virginia Creeper (*Vitis quinquefolia*)*. This requires support. It makes dense growth in a short space of time. Ideal for nesting sites.

There are, of course, many more plants suitable for growing in aviaries and I would suggest that you refer to one of the many gardening books available if the plants you would like in your aviary are not included above.

A word of warning. Certain plants, due to their poisonous nature, are not suitable for aviaries; indeed, certain species, such as laburnums (*Laburnum*), should not be grown anywhere near an aviary as the seeds are highly toxic. Certain bulbs can also prove toxic, as can foxgloves (*Digitalis* spp.). If in doubt, then read up on the plant *before* including it in your aviary.

PLUM-HEADED FINCH
(*Aidemosyne modesta*) (color photos on pages 126–127)
The overall length is approximately 110 mm (4⅓ in). The adult cock has the forehead, crown, and chin dull plum-red. The hind neck to rump, including wings, is brown, with the wing and tail coverts edged with white. The tail is black, as are the lores. The sides of the face and throat to the under-tail coverts are dull white, barred, mainly on the breast and flanks, with brown. The hen is similar but lacks the red on the chin and also has prominent white eye-stripes which extend well past the eyes. The beak is black.

The species is found from central northern Queensland, around Atherton and Townsville, down through central New South Wales to the northern Riverina district and Canberra. There is a seasonal migration, with birds moving north in the winter and south during the summer. The preferred habitat is savannah grassland, where this species is most often seen feeding on or near the ground in tall grass, reeds, and bushes alongside the margins of creeks, rivers, and lagoons.

This easily sexed species also goes by the name of Cherry Finch. Although never as popular with aviculturists as many of the other Australian finches (due no doubt to its rather modest garb), it does have its admirers, and numbers have never become so low as to endanger its existence in aviculture. It is a very quiet bird and is not aggressive in a mixed collection. Colony breeding in a

Bicheno Finches (1)

Bicheno Finch –
Black-rumped race.
This excellent
photograph shows
the black rump to
advantage. Other
than when birds are
in flight, it is
difficult to see the
rump color on a
Bicheno Finch, as,
at rest, the wings
cover most of the
rump area.

Plum-headed
Finches at three
weeks of age.

A Plum-headed
Finch in immature
plumage.

large indoor flight or outside aviary has proved successful, however one may come across the occasional cock bird that proves extremely aggressive to others of his own sex and kind. Such a bird can cause havoc in a colony and may have to be removed if successful breeding results are to be realized.

The Plum-headed Finch is often reported as being somewhat sensitive with regard to choice of partners and it is suggested that a number of pairs should be housed together to enable the birds to pair up naturally. Personally, I have not found this to be the case and pairs which I have particularly wanted to use together have taken to each other without any problems arising. It is also repeatedly mentioned that the Plum-headed Finch is excessively nervous when incubating, particularly during the first few days. Again, I have not found this to be the case; indeed, I regard the Plum-headed as being far less nervous when incubating than the Star Finch. Nevertheless, as both of these statements are made regularly, often by extremely experienced breeders, there can obviously be 'problems' with the Plum-headed and the newcomer should take heed of such warnings.

If housed in an aviary, the Plum-headed must have a heated shelter to which it can retire during inclement weather conditions. It would also prove beneficial to successful breeding if the birds could be persuaded to use nest boxes in the shelter, rather than be allowed to build their own nests in the shrubs or bushes in the flight area. The species takes well to cage life and will breed successfully in a large box cage. The clutch usually consists of between four and seven eggs. Incubation usually commences after the second or third egg is laid, with the cock and hen taking turns during the day but only the latter staying on the nest during the night. The chicks hatch after approximately 12 days and remain in the nest for three weeks.

Upon fledging, they are dull olive-brown on the upperparts, with grayish-white underparts which have little or no barring. Sexing is possible after approximately eight weeks, when the youngsters begin their molt from immature to adult plumage, as at this stage the bib of the young males becomes evident. Full adult plumage is attained after about four months. At this time, the sexes should be split up and housed separately, otherwise one may find that certain cock birds will become extremely aggressive toward their siblings if the sexes are left together. Another reason for segregating the sexes is to enable the youngsters to develop fully before coming into breeding condition.

Plum-headed Finches will successfully rear their young on a diet of seeds alone. However, live food should be offered in the hope that the birds will take it. Soaked seeds are relished and should be supplied freely, as should a good quality soft food. Just before egg-laying commences, both sexes will take large quantities of flaked cuttlefish bone, although why the cock birds should feel the need for this, I have no idea!

At present there is only one mutation, namely the Fawn (or Isobel, as it is often called). At the time of writing, few are available in either the USA or the UK, although it is present in some numbers in Europe and can also be found in Australia. From all accounts, it is a sex-linked mutation (see GENETICS).

PURCHASING STOCK
The ideal way in which to obtain good breeding stock is to approach a successful breeder. The names and addresses of such people are usually to be found in the members list of a specialist society or club. Alternatively, breeding stock can be found in the advertisement columns of commercially published journals devoted to aviculture.

Most serious breeders of Australian finches keep strict records of the birds they breed, and a potential purchaser can usually obtain full details of the birds he or she is about to buy. For those who wish to linebreed, full details of parentage should be asked for, especially if mutations are being purchased. If potential stock is closed-banded, it is possible to ascertain the year in which the birds were born by the color code (and date stamp) on the band. However, it is beneficial to

Plum-headed Finch (cock).

Bicheno Finches (2)

Bicheno Finch (hen) – Black-rumped race. Due partly to the Black-rumped race being recessive to the White-rumped, numbers of the former became very low in the UK and only in recent times have sufficient enthusiasts taken up the breeding of the Black-rumped Bicheno to ensure its availability for future aviculturists.

Bicheno Finch – White-rumped race. The Bicheno Finch, although attired only in black, brown and white, is, nevertheless, most attractive. The species is extremely difficult to sex by visual means. However, the author found that by placing birds on their own for a while the cocks could be persuaded to sing. This method of sexing is now used by the majority of breeders.

Red-browed Finch. This species is commonly known as the Sydney Waxbill. This is a complete misnomer as it is far more widely distributed than the Sydney area and is not a waxbill but a true Australian grassfinch.

Due no doubt to its resemblance to certain African waxbills, it is not a popular species with aviculturists. In Australia it is looked upon by many as being rather dull and unattractive. It is also extremely difficult to sex visually.

ask the breeder for the exact date of birth.

Only healthy birds should be purchased; any showing signs of ill-health being left strictly alone. Birds with overgrown or crossed beaks should not be bought, as they often prove unreliable for breeding due to their inability to feed young correctly. One should also be wary of purchasing birds that are not closed-banded, as if such birds are not from a reputable breeder, there is no way of knowing their exact age.

If young stock is purchased, then only take those birds which are in full adult plumage. This is especially important where Gouldian Finches are concerned, as the stress caused by the move could kill a Gouldian which is in immature or partly immature plumage. The move will almost certainly affect the molting process, not only in Gouldians but in all Australian finch youngsters.

I prefer to handle most of the birds I am considering purchasing before a deal is concluded. If you feel a little apprehensive about taking hold of a bird, then ask the owner to hold the bird while you inspect it. Check that it is firmly fleshed but not fat, especially along the breast. Also check that there is no soiling around the area of the vent, and that the eyes and nostrils are clean and free from infection.

The majority of breeders feed their birds as described under DIET. Nevertheless, it would be prudent to ask the breeder from whom you are about to purchase birds exactly what diet his or her birds have been used to. If it differs in any way from the one you will be offering, then watch the birds closely for a few days. If they appear stressed in any way, check that they are, in fact, taking the foods offered. If they are not, then you should immediately offer the same diet used by the breeder from whom you obtained them. You can then, over a period, persuade them to take the diet you normally give your own birds. The main thing is to get them settled into their new quarters before any attempts are made to alter the diet on which they were raised. (See also TRANSPORTATION.)

QUARANTINE
Nowadays most countries insist on imported birds going through a period of quarantine before being released to the trade or directly to their new owners. Even though such birds will have gone through a period of quarantine, they should still be kept separate from your original stock for at least three to four weeks. In fact, no matter where birds are purchased from, they should never be placed immediately in the same quarters as your own birds. I do not suggest that newly purchased Australian finches need to be housed in a separate building, but they should, however, be caged on their own for at least three to four weeks.

If the birds are destined for aviaries, they should still be caged for the period suggested. Over the three- to four-week period, the birds should be observed regularly to ensure that there are no signs of disease and that they have taken to the diet supplied. Should any show signs of being unwell, then raising the temperature of the birdroom a little is often all that is required to bring them back into condition.

Birds that have been cage-bred will require extra attention if they are eventually to be housed in an aviary, and neither these nor aviary-bred stock should be released into aviary accommodation during the colder months of the year, but should remain caged until weather conditions are more suitable.

R

RECORD-KEEPING

If you wish to linebreed, then it is essential that strict records of your birds are kept. Commercially produced record cards or books are obtainable from most suppliers of cage bird requisites. Alternatively, you could make use of a notebook with a page devoted to each breeding pair. Should you decide on the latter method, spaces would be required for incubation dates, hatching, number of chicks reared, band numbers, sex of youngsters, and, if mutations are bred, the type of mutation. Only by keeping strict records can a breeder hope to improve his or her stock over the years.

I have found it most beneficial to devote a page to all the youngsters that are successfully reared to independence each season. If more than one species is being bred, then a page should be given over to each individual species rather than entering youngsters from different species on the same page. Using this method, at the end of the breeding season you will be able to see at a glance how many chicks have been reared and from which breeding pairs the chicks have come.

This can be of great help when you are deciding which birds should be paired together the following season. Also, if chicks which have been sold are recorded as such, you will be able to see at a glance which birds have been retained.

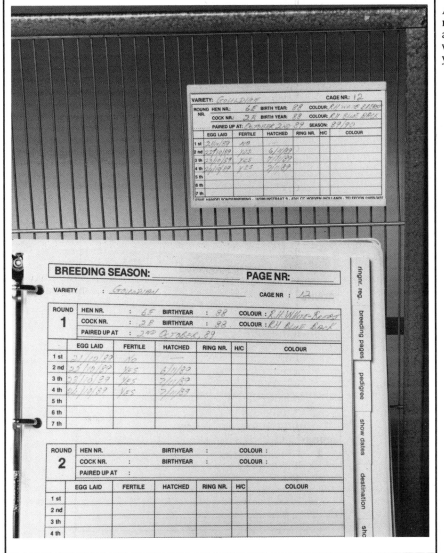

A record card and record book, which are essential if you wish to line-breed your birds.

Plum-headed Finch

Plum-headed Finch (cock) – Fawn (or Isobel) mutation. This is a relatively new mutation and, as yet, little is known of its genetic make-up. It is believed to be a sex-linked mutation.

Plum-headed Finch pair (cock on left). This species is often given the name Cherry Finch. Although it has no bright colors, its markings are attractive and, if housed in a mixed collection of Australian finches, it is a perfect foil to the more colorful species.
Being easy to sex and fairly easy to breed in both cage and aviary accommodation, it can prove an ideal species for the newcomer to Australian finches.

Plum-headed Finch (hen) – Fawn (or Isobel) mutation.
If this bird is compared with the cock opposite, it will be seen how easily the species can be sexed.

Plum-headed Finch in immature plumage.
It is possible to sex young Plum-headed Finches at a fairly early age, as they begin to molt from immature to adult plumage when they are some eight weeks of age. At this stage of their development, the bib of the cock birds becomes evident.

RED-BROWED FINCH (*Aegintha temporalis*) (color photo on page 123)
The approximate overall length is some 101 mm (4 in). Adults are gray on the top of the head, extending to the nape, with a broad stripe of red on the lores and superciliary. The sides of the head and neck are pale gray; the back and wings olive; the rump and upper-tail coverts crimson. The tail is dark brown; the underparts are whitish with a buff-ash wash on the flanks. The beak is red, with a triangular black patch on the culmen and on the center of the lower mandible.

After the Zebra Finch, the Red-browed is the most widely distributed Australian finch. It is found from Cape York Peninsula around the eastern and southern coastlines, to the Mount Lofty Ranges near Adelaide in South Australia. Recently it has been introduced into the Perth area. The species can be found in a variety of habitats, from the edge of rain forest to damp eucalypt woodland. It can also be found in open forest, heath, mangrove, orchards, and in parks and gardens in the heart of urban areas.

The Red-browed Finch is more commonly known as the Sydney Waxbill in the UK. This is a complete misnomer as it is far more widely distributed than the Sydney area and is not a waxbill but a true Australian grassfinch!

It is not a popular species with aviculturists. In the UK this is no doubt due to its resemblance to an African waxbill; in Australia it is looked upon by many as rather dull and unattractive. Also, it is common in the wild and inexpensive to purchase in Australia, which is far from the case elsewhere! It is often recommended that aviary accommodation is the most suitable for this species, however the person who has had the greatest success with this species in the UK has always housed his breeding pairs in cages.

Although not essential, it is recommended that breeding pairs with young be offered live food; green food is also taken in quantity. Soaked seeds and some form of soft food would also prove beneficial to the successful rearing of chicks.

Sexing is extremely difficult with this species. Cocks are reported as having an eyebrow stripe which extends further behind the eye than that of the hen; it is also squarer at the end. Immature birds have dull crimson rumps and lack the eyebrow stripe; their beaks are black.

The clutch consists of from four to six eggs. A habit which is common to most groups of passerine birds, but is exceptionally rare in grassfinches, is that Red-browed youngsters quiver their wings when begging for food. Young birds molt into adult plumage within 10 to 12 weeks of age, when they become identical to their parents. Therefore, if the breeding adults are housed in aviary accommodation, it is imperative that the youngsters either be fitted with closed-bands or, if this is not possible, with plastic split bands. Alternatively, they could be removed from their parents the moment they become independent. Left with the parents, it would prove almost impossible to distinguish the youngsters from the adults once they had molted into adult plumage.

Red-brows form a strong pair bond and, in the wild at least, mate for life. In the wild an 'orange' and a 'yellow' phase occur naturally. In Australia these have been reproduced under captive conditions. The beak, brow, rump, and upper-tail coverts are dull orange or a light golden-yellow in the orange and yellow mutations, respectively.

RED-EARED FIRETAIL (*Emblema oculata*)
The approximate overall length is 115 mm (4½ in). From forehead to lower back and wings, the Red-eared Firetail is olive-brown, finely barred with blackish-brown; the rump and upper-tail coverts are bright crimson-red; the tail is olivaceous, barred with black, crimson at the base and along the outer edges. From chin to breast the plumage is pale buffish-gray, finely barred with black; the lores and line around the eyes are black, with a small bright-red patch behind each eye. The abdomen and flanks to under the tail are black spotted with white. The beak is red and the eye-rings are pale blue.

When not breeding, the sexes

128

are alike. In breeding condition, the cock is brighter in color with a scarlet ear-spot, while that of the hen is orange.

The Red-eared Firetail is found only in the southwest of the state of Western Australia, in a pocket along the Darling Range, stretching across the plateau from the town of Esperance to north of Perth on the opposite coast. It inhabits dense heath and thick undergrowth in gullies and forests, where it nests in trees and shrubs up to 15 m (48 ft) above the ground.

It appears the species was first bred in captivity by Dr. M. Chinner of Adelaide in 1938. In 1960, Alwyn Pepper (Scarborough, Western Australia) obtained four eggs from a fallen nest in the wild. The eggs were placed under Society Finch fosters and two young, a cock and a hen, were successfully reared. These two birds formed a mated pair and bred in their first year. Mr. Pepper continued to breed from these birds and their offspring, and in 1986 he received an award from the Avicultural Society of Australia for his study of the species. A detailed article on the Red-eared Firetail by Mr. Pepper appeared in *Cage and Aviary Birds* in 1966.

At the present time the Red-eared Firetail is not available to aviculturists outside Australia.

RINGED FINCH (see BICHENO FINCH)

RODENTS, CONTROL OF
Due to the nature of the foods they eat, birds invariably attract rats, mice, and other vermin. Such creatures carry disease and if they are able to foul the birds' food with their droppings or urine, then disease will almost certainly spread among one's stock. Rats and mice will also consume the birds' food and the former may even kill the birds, especially young still in the nest. At the least, such vermin, if allowed entry to the birds' quarters, will greatly disturb the occupants during the night, thus causing breeding pairs to desert their eggs or young.

It is extremely difficult to make aviaries rodentproof. Only if the enclosures have concrete floors and the wire is no more than 9 mm (⅜ in) mesh, with no gaps whatsoever, could the enclosures be considered free from invasion.

If vermin do gain access to your aviaries, immediate action must be taken. Poison or traps should be placed in containers which the birds would find impossible to enter. However, with a plentiful supply of food always at hand, it is doubtful if the poison would be taken. Break-back traps have the disadvantage of catching only one rodent at a setting. By far the most superior trap is one that will allow any number of rodents to enter, but from which, once inside, they would find it impossible to escape. Such traps are usually birdproof and can be placed in any position in the flight or shelter. Each morning the traps can be inspected and any rodents caught can either be drowned by placing the trap in a bucket of water or, for those who dislike killing any form of life, the occupants can be released into the countryside, preferably many miles from where they were trapped!

It is not so difficult to make a birdroom verminproof. However, should rodents gain entry, they can cause as much havoc as they would in an aviary and traps should be set immediately to try to eliminate the pests.

A favorite place for mice to gather in a birdroom is between the insulating panels and the outside walls or roof. If some form of insulating material has been placed between the inside panel and the outer wall or roof, mice will nest in this. Unless something is done to eradicate the vermin, the birdroom will soon become overrun. A serious infestation of rodents could mean that the birdroom would have to be emptied of all birds and cages and the insulating panels removed. Once clear of vermin, the panels could be replaced, and any entry holes made by the rodents securely plugged.

S

SEED

Information on seed requirements for Australian finches will be found under DIET. It should, however, be emphasized that only the best quality seed you can afford should be purchased and only those seeds advertised as being already cleaned should be offered to your stock.

If you are able to examine the seeds before you purchase them, ask to be shown a sample and sift this through your fingers. If dust, dirt, or husks cling to your fingers after handling the seeds, then you can be certain the seeds have not been cleaned properly and you should ask to see another sample or take your business elsewhere. Good-quality seeds should have a plump, highly polished appearance. If the seeds offered for your inspection have a somewhat withered or dehydrated look, then they are far from fresh and should not be purchased. Care must be taken when buying mixtures of seeds (such as foreign-finch mixture) as very often too much of one type of seed may have been added to the mixture (usually white or panicum millet) and if such a mixture is fed exclusively to your birds, they will not receive a balanced diet.

Many aviculturists (especially those with large collections) purchase the seeds they require by mail order. If you decide to purchase seed in this way, ensure that you deal with a reputable firm. One whose advertisements regularly appear in the fancy press is almost certain to be reliable.

SEEDING GRASSES

For birds housed in aviaries and/or indoor flights, seeding grasses, when in season, can be offered. They should be securely tied in small bundles and hung near to perches where the birds will have easy access to them.

Obviously, caged birds also relish these grasses, however problems may be encountered if such grasses are supplied throughout the breeding season, as cock birds may, after feeding on the grasses, attempt to remove individual stalks and carry them into the nest. If the birds continue to do this, the eggs could eventually be covered and the breeding pair would then almost certainly desert.

There is little doubt that all Australian finches enjoy picking over seeding grasses, and if they are available outside of the breeding season, by all means offer them to your birds. It is essential that such grasses be taken from an area free from fouling by dogs and cats, and one should also ensure that the area has not been sprayed with insecticides or polluted in any other way. If in doubt, then do not offer seeding grasses at all. A good alternative is SOAKED SEEDS.

SELLING STOCK

From time to time a successful bird keeper will no doubt have surplus birds he or she wishes to dispose of. Do remember, when selling surplus birds to other bird keepers, especially if they are new to the hobby, to be as fair as possible in your dealings. If your birds are fitted with closed-bands, then the would-be purchaser will be able to see at a glance how old the birds are (although a newcomer may have to be told that the color of the band denotes the year the bird was born). If you do not fit closed-bands, then it is to be hoped that you will still have records of when the birds were born. It is also important to inform the would-be purchaser of the sex of the birds. If this is not known, then do tell the person concerned that you are selling the birds as unsexed. You should also divulge the parentage of the birds; if they are related, then emphasize the fact. Many would-be buyers will also wish to know if the birds were parent- or foster-reared.

Usually a successful breeder will, at the end of each breeding season, have surplus young to sell. No doubt he or she will also have a few older pairs to dispose of. Normally I only keep a bird for two seasons, no matter how well the bird has performed in the breeding pen. This means that when I sell such birds, the purchaser can expect at least one good breeding season from the bird in question. If the buyer is told this before making

A small cage that is ideal for transporting Australian finches. The cage is also suitable for displaying birds for sale.

purchase, then there should be no comeback when the birds, after one season, fail to breed as well as they did when they were younger. With these older birds, I usually ask a little less than I would for a first-year bird.

If you are fair in your dealings, you can be almost certain that fellow bird keepers will be keen to purchase stock from you and, in addition, they will pass the word around that birds purchased from you are exactly as described.

Many clubs and/or societies now hold selling days where, for a small entrance fee, a bird keeper can take his or her surplus stock. Remember, if you do decide to dispose of your birds in this way, to place them in suitable cages which are roomy and *clean*. At some of these sale days, I have seen birds housed in cramped cages which have obviously not been cleaned since they were last used. Is it any wonder the birds remained unsold?

If you are unable to attend society sale days, then you can, of course, advertise your surplus birds either in a commercial periodical devoted to bird-keeping or, as is often possible, in the journal of the society/club of which you are a member.

When advertising birds for sale, be prepared to spend a little extra money on a full description rather than just stating the species and the price. If you are not willing to send the birds by road or rail, then state this in your advertisement. It is also a good idea (when advertising in commercial journals) not to give your full address (just your first name and telephone number will suffice), otherwise you may be troubled by visitors at unsuitable times, or, what is even worse, you may be visited by bird thieves rather than prospective purchasers!

SEXING
Of the 18 species of Australian finch, 11 are monomorphic, i.e., the sexes are virtually identical. This can cause problems and is most probably one of the main reasons why many supposed 'pairs' do not breed. Two cock birds housed together will often refuse to sing, and as they may be seen to enter the nest box regularly and even roost in it, although no eggs are forthcoming, their owner may leave them together for some time in the belief that they are a true pair.

Two hens housed together will eventually begin to lay eggs and, upon inspecting the nest box, anything up to 12 eggs may be found. You can then be certain that both birds are, in fact, hens.

Many bird keepers attempt to sex monomorphic species by visual means (see MONOMORPHIC SPECIES), but with the majority the differences are very slight. Unless you have considerable experience with the species concerned, it can prove an almost impossible task and even an experienced person may be fooled by an exceptionally well-marked hen or a poorly colored cock bird.

The most reliable method of sexing is to use the cock's song as an indication. With the majority of species, young cock birds will begin to sing soon after weaning. If young birds are studied regularly, then any seen to sing can be caught up. If closed-banded, the band number can be recorded or, better still, a colored split band can be fitted and one can then tell at a glance the sex of each individual bird.

Unfortunately, Bicheno cocks, if housed with others of either sex, rarely sing, even when young. However, a method which I have found to be most reliable is to house such birds on their own for a while. If the lone bird is a cock, it will begin to sing within minutes. To persuade the bird to sing almost immediately, it needs to be placed on its own in a cage similar to that which it has been used to. If your young birds are housed in large flight cages which can be partitioned off (see CAGES), then it is a simple matter to segregate one bird at a time, give it the opportunity to show its sex, and, once it has, to remove it to a holding cage until all the birds in the flight cage have been sexed. If this is not possible, then each individual bird will have to be given time to settle into its new surrounding before it can be sexed, but even then it should take no more than, say, five minutes for a cock to commence singing.

Young birds housed in aviaries or indoor flights would, of course, have to be caught and caged before attempting to sex them. Such birds should be given a day or so to settle before any such attempt is made. A further point is most important. No bird which you are attempting to sex by using the above method should be placed in a show cage, as the bird may take hours to settle in such a cage and even then it may not sing, whether or not it is a cock.

The method described is most reliable when attempting to determine the sex of Bicheno Finches. It can also be used with certain other species, such as Long-tailed Grassfinches (and Heck's), also Black-throated (Parson), and Masked. However, with most young cock birds (other than Bichenos), even if a number are housed together, they will begin to sing shortly after being weaned. By the time they begin their molt from immature to adult plumage, they will sing almost continuously.

I have not been able to sex Australian mannikins using the method described for Bicheno Finches, but as young mannikin cocks will almost certainly sing when housed with others of their kind, there should be few problems in determining the sex of individuals. This also applies to the Society Finch.

**SHAFT-TAILED GRASSFINCH
(see LONG-TAILED GRASSFINCH)**

SHOW CAGE (see EXHIBITING)

SOAKED SEEDS
In my opinion it is essential that soaked (or to give them the correct, but rarely used term, germinated) seeds be supplied freely to all Australian finches when they have young in the nest. I have yet to find a breeding pair that refuses to take these seeds; indeed, some pairs will, for a time, feed them almost exclusively to their offspring. Seeds which have just begun to sprout appear to be the ones most favored by the birds; well-sprouted seeds are often ignored and those showing no signs of sprouting are only picked over.

Certain seeds do not sprout as quickly as others. Although some breeders offer soaked foreign-finch mixture, I have always found 50/50 budgerigar mixture (i.e., 50 percent white millet and 50 percent plain canary seed) to be the ideal. Alternatively, you could mix your own soaked seeds using equal parts of plain canary seed to equal parts of white millet.

To ensure a constant supply of soaked seeds, carry out the following procedure. Enough seed for one day's feeding should be placed in a clean plastic sieve. The sieve should then be placed inside a 500-g (1 lb) margarine tub (or something similar) and lukewarm water should be added until it reaches the top of the tub. The tub should then be placed inside

Seeds being soaked.

another container (a 12-cm [5-in] plastic flowerpot saucer being ideal) in case of water spillage, and the whole set-up should then be placed on a shelf in the birdroom, or somewhere similar, where it will be in a fairly warm place but will not become liable to contamination. The seed should be left to soak for a period of two days, during which time the water is emptied away, the seeds are rinsed under a running tap, and fresh water is added at least twice.

When the soaking period is completed, the seeds should be given a final rinse under a running tap, left to drain for a quarter of an hour, then tipped into a clean 12-cm (5 in) flowerpot saucer (or suchlike), which is itself covered with a saucer of the same size. The seeds should then be left in a fairly warm position for 24 hours, after which they should be ready for use. To have a continual supply of soaked seeds, two sieves are required, one always being used a day in advance of the other, plus two margarine tubs and four 12-cm (5 in) saucers.

If all the seeds from one soaking are not used at once, they must be covered, otherwise they will quickly dry out and much of their attraction for the birds will be lost. All the seeds from one soaking should be used the same day. Any left over should be discarded, as by the following morning the seeds will have sprouted to such an extent that they will no longer prove attractive to the birds.

I find 250 g (½ lb) of seed is enough for a breeding stud comprising eight to ten pairs, plus

Soaked seeds. Left: soaking seeds just after they have been placed in the saucers. Right: soaked seeds that have already sprouted and are ready for feeding to your birds.

their chicks. For larger studs, more soaked seeds would, of course, be required. The procedure, however, is exactly the same.

SOCIETIES
Listed in this entry are a selection of finch societies and the main national avicultural organizations that have an interest in finches and, in particular, Australian finches. Any of these will be a good source of information, or alternatively may help you to contact a local or specialized group in your own area.

AUSTRALIA
The Avicultural Society of Australia, Inc., 52 Harris Road, Elliminyt, Victoria 3249.
Journal: *Australian Aviculture*
Secretary/Editor: Graeme Hyde

Queensland Finch Society Inc.
Journal: *Finch News Magazine*
Editor: Russell Kingston, P. O. Box 303, Woollongalba, Queensland 4102.

Journal: *Western Australian Avicultural Magazine*
Editor: Mrs D. Payne, 138 Queens Road, South Guildford, Western Australia 6055.

CANADA
Avicultural Advancement Council of Canada, P. O. Box 5126, Station B, Victoria, BC V8R 6N4.

DENMARK
Journal: *Dansk Fuglehold*, Faergevej 17, Postboks 101, DK 3600 Frederikssund.

FEDERAL REPUBLIC OF GERMANY
Journal: *Gefiederte Welt*, Verlag Eugen Ulmer GmbH & Co., Wollgvasweg 41, Postfach 70 05 61 D-7000 Stuttgart 70.

ITALY
Club dell' Esotico
Secretary: Giovanni Agostini, Via Mario Gordini 15, 47100 Forli Fo, Italy.

NETHERLANDS
Nederlandse Bond van Vogelliefhebbers
Journal: *Onze Vogels*, P. O. Box 74, Bergen op Zoom.

NEW ZEALAND
The Avicultural Society of New Zealand, P. O. Box 21403, Henderson, Auckland 8.

SINGAPORE
Singapore Avicultural Society, 1 Goldhill Plaza, Podium Block, 03–43, Singapore 1130.

SOUTH AFRICA
Avicultural Council of Southern Africa, Dr. W. D. Russell, P. O. Box 65188, Benmore, 2010.

South African National Cage Bird Association, Mr F. Barnicoat, P. O. Box 40108, Cleveland, 2022 Transvaal.

Avicultural Research Unit, c/o Neville Brickell, 100 Innes Road, Durban 4001, Natal.

UNITED KINGDOM
Avicultural Society
Secretary: Mary Harvey, Warren Hill, Hulfords Lane, Hartley Wintney, Hampshire RG27 8AG.

Australian Finch Society,
Secretary: J. Kidd, 3 Newbigging Cottages, Luthermuir, Laurencekirk, Kincardineshire.

Foreign Bird League
Secretaries: Mr and Mrs C. W. Stevens, Monks Cottage, 58 Preston Crowmarsh, Benson, Oxon, OX9 6SL.

USA
American Federation of Aviculture.
Journal: *The AFS Watchbird*
Membership Services: P. O. Box 56218, Phoenix, AZ 85079–6218.

Avicultural Society of America
Membership Secretary: Helen Hanson, Riverside, CA 92517.

SOCIETY FINCH (see BENGALESE FINCH)

SOFT FOOD
Many species of Australian finch, especially when rearing young, can be persuaded to take a good proprietary brand of soft food. One of the brands most extensively used in the UK and in Europe is Cé-Dé, a Dutch product. In the United States L/M Universal Plus and L/M Canary, Finch and Softbill Plus are also quite popular as is Cé-Dé.
Whatever brand is used, it should be mixed exactly as per the instructions on the package and should be neither too dry nor too moist. Such foods can be supplied

freely when chicks are in the nest, and if the parent birds will continue to feed these foods to their chicks up until weaning, then so much the better. However, once the chicks have been removed from their parents, the supply of soft food should be discontinued until the birds again have chicks. To supply soft food to pairs which are incubating may stimulate them into wanting to nest again before the incubation period is completed. The eggs would then be deserted, especially if the cock bird began to pester the hen because of overstimulation.

The soft food should be mixed fresh each morning and any left over after a 24-hour period should be discarded (it could be put out for wild birds as they, no doubt, would appreciate such offerings). It is entirely up to the breeder whether he or she offers the soft food in a separate dish, or places it, as I do, in the same dish as the soaked seeds. I do not place the soft food directly on top of the soaked seeds, but keep it to one side of the dish. Offering soft food in this way can often persuade pairs that would not normally take such food to at least sample it, as a certain amount would be taken when eating the soaked seeds.

Another form of soft food which can be offered to Australian finches is the type known as insectivorous food. Although more often associated with softbilled birds than finches, many Australian finches will sample these foods, and some will often take large amounts when they have chicks in the nest. The majority of such foods do not require mixing with water (as do Cé-Dé), but can be fed straight from the package. This type of food also has a longer cage life than Cé-Dé, but even so, if it is not eaten within a day or so of being offered, or becomes fouled in any way, it should immediately be discarded.

Very often insectivorous food is offered to the birds in small finger drawers attached to the cage front, rather than being placed in a dish on the cage floor. For aviary birds, however, such food would have to be supplied in a small dish on the feeding station, alongside the other foods.

It is always worth experimenting with different types of soft food, especially if one is attempting to raise chicks of a species which is notoriously difficult to breed from. Supplying a soft food which the birds actually like and will feed to their chicks can make the difference between success and failure!

SPLIT BANDS (RINGS)
These bands are made of plastic and can be obtained in self-colors

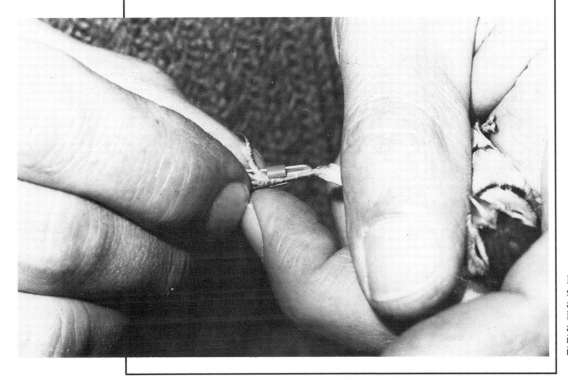

Fitting a plastic split band on an adult Bicheno Finch. Such bands are ideal for identifying individual birds.

or in a combination of two colors with either narrow or broad stripes. If required, they can also be inlaid with numbers, usually running consecutively. As they can be fitted to a bird of any age, they prove invaluable for identification of parentage, gender, etc.

I always fit closed-bands to all the Australian finches I breed, nevertheless I find split bands to be extremely useful, especially with species in which the sexes are monomorphic, as if these bands are fitted one can tell the sex of a bird at a glance. For instance, when I determine the sex of any monomorphic species I have bred, I always, at the same time, fit a colored split band on the cock birds, leaving the hens with only their closed-bands as a means of identification.

If, for some reason, a breeder is unable to closed-band chicks, then split bands can be fitted to all the birds at the time of weaning. To enable you to keep records correctly, a self-colored, numbered split ring could be placed on one leg. The color could denote the parentage of each chick and the number could be used to identify each individual chick. If the chicks are of a species which is monomorphic, then the cocks (or hens if the breeder prefers), when sexed, could be fitted with a different colored split band on the opposite leg.

Split bands are also useful for identifying adult birds that have not been fitted with closed-bands. Therefore, if newly purchased birds are not fitted with any type of band, it is a good idea to fit split bands immediately before the birds are placed in their new quarters.

There is not such a wide choice of sizes in plastic split bands as there is in aluminum closed-bands. It is suggested by band manufacturers that size XF is suitable for all the Australian finches except for the Chestnut-breasted, Pictorella, and Yellow-rumped Finches. For these three species, size XCS is recommended. This size is also recommended for the Diamond Firetail.

I have found that size XF is, in fact, too large for Bicheno Finches, as when the birds commence breeding the split band is often lost while the birds are incubating. It is sometimes possible to purchase smaller split bands than size XF, and if you are able to locate such bands, I would suggest that you use these on Bicheno Finches. If you are unable to find a smaller split band than size XF, I can only suggest that if the split bands are lost during the breeding season, you fit split bands again once breeding is finished, as it is only during incubation that the birds appear to lose these bands.

As mentioned above, size XCS is suggested as suitable for Australian mannikins. However, I have always found size XF to be suitable. This size of split band can also be fitted to Society Finches.

SPRAY MILLET
Although not an essential part of the diet, spray millet is relished by all Australian finches and it can be offered as often as you wish. My birds have a supply available at all times.

For caged birds, the sprays can be placed in a clip which is attached to the cage front. To save cluttering the cage front with numerous clips, however, I have devised a method whereby the sprays can be attached to the back wall of the cage (see illustration). This also helps to keep the husks from the sprays at the rear of the cage, thus avoiding the tendency for them to be blown out onto the birdroom floor by the movement of the birds.

It is wasteful to supply caged birds with a complete spray and I always cut them into pieces of approximately 9 cm (3½ in) in length before offering them to the birds. Each time I feed the birds I rotate the sprays, until the whole piece is stripped of seed, when it is then discarded.

For birds housed in flights and/or aviaries, sprays can be suspended in small bundles. The birds will cling to these when taking the seeds.

Many bird keepers offer soaked sprays which have been placed in water for a day or so until they show signs of sprouting. As with soaked seeds, the water in which the sprays are immersed requires changing regularly. Once the sprays show signs of sprouting, they should be given a thorough rinsing before being offered to the birds.

Sprays of millet hung over a perch in an aviary.

A spray millet holder as designed and used by the author. This type of holder can be attached to the rear wall of a cage.

STAR FINCH (*Neochmia ruficauda*) (color photos on pages 58–59, 62–63)

The approximate length is 110 mm (4¼ in). Adult cocks have the entire front of the head, ear coverts, and throat crimson. The ear coverts, mesia, and throat are profusely spotted with white. From nape to rump and the wings the plumage is olive. The upper-tail coverts are dull carmine; the breast and flanks olivaceous-gray, each feather having a subterminal white spot. The abdomen is yellowish-white; the under-tail coverts are white. The beak is bright red.

Adult hens are similar to the cock but the white spotting is not so prominent and the red on the facial area is less extensive.

This species is found in northern Australia, from the Pilbara region in Western Australia, through the Kimberley range and the Northern Territory, across Arnham Land to Cape York and northern Queensland. It appears, however, that the species has suffered a serious decline, with the Queensland population, in particular, now very scarce. The habitat includes reeds and tall grasses alongside creeks and rivers in eucalypt woodland. It can also be found near mangroves.

Sometimes referred to as the Ruficauda Finch, the Star Finch is one of the most popular of Australian finches, both with the beginner and the more experienced enthusiast. It is also one of the least expensive. Sexing of *adult* birds is easy; however, before the sexes can be determined accurately, the birds usually need to be nine months or more of age. Young cocks can be sexed at an earlier age as the majority start to sing shortly after becoming independent. However, unless strict observation is carried out, one could not guarantee that nonsinging birds are in fact hens until they attain their full adult plumage.

Stars readily take to a conventional-style nest box (see NEST BOXES) and they will breed readily in aviary accommodation, cages, or indoor flights. They will also mix well with other species which are of approximately the same size.

Few pairs will attempt to build a

137

Star Finches at three weeks of age.

nest from scratch, therefore the nest box should be filled with soft hay before placing it in position. A certain amount of nesting material should, however, be placed within easy reach of the breeding pair and a supply should always be on hand at least until the chicks have hatched, otherwise the cock bird may, through boredom, remove material from the nest, in some cases so depleting the nest that the hen deserts.

The average clutch is five or six eggs and incubation usually begins after the fourth egg is laid. Once the hen begins to incubate in earnest, the cock is rarely allowed to remain on the nest with her during the night. However, he may be allowed to do so once the chicks have hatched. Incubation varies from between 12 to 15 days. Stars are light sitters and even the most steady of pairs will leave the nest at the least provocation. Both birds will take their turn at incubation, but it is the hen who does most.

A Star Finch — Pied mutation at three weeks of age. Note the beak which, at this age, is white with a few black markings. When the bird molts into sub-adult plumage the beak becomes red, masking the white area completely.

As Star Finches are such light sitters, nest inspection is easily carried out as the least disturbance will often persuade the incubating bird to vacate the nest. However, as this species is less tolerant of nest inspection than many Australian finches, I would suggest the eggs be inspected for fertility only once, the best time being seven or eight days after incubation begins. If the eggs (or the majority of them) prove fertile, do not inspect the nest again until the chicks are approximately nine to ten days of age. At this age, well-fed chicks should be ready to be closed-banded.

Most Stars will rear their chicks successfully on a diet of seeds alone, however it is beneficial to offer other foods. Some pairs may be persuaded to accept live food and most breeding pairs will take a good quality soft food. Star Finch chicks fledge at approximately 20 days of age. For the first few days they may prove extremely nervous, even when the parent birds are steady. At this stage of their development, therefore, you should attend to their needs as unobtrusively as possible. After a week or so, the youngsters will have become more confiding, and by the time they are independent they should be as settled as the parent birds.

Immature Star Finches have the upperparts dull olive-brown with the underparts brownish-buff, fading to white on the lower breast and turning to pure white on the abdomen and under-tail coverts. The beak is black; the legs and feet are brown. Young Stars begin to molt into subadult plumage at approximately eight weeks of age. When this molt is completed, the birds look very much like poorly colored adults. The cocks will have a certain amount of red on the face and head, but not nearly so much as a fully adult bird. The overall body color is paler than in an adult, with less prominent white spotting. Hens in subadult plumage have only a few red feathers on the forehead; the overall color is much paler than that of the cocks. The beaks of both sexes turn from black to red, and the legs and the feet become yellow.

It may be seven or eight months before the birds again begin to molt. When this is completed, the birds will then be in full adult plumage. With each subsequent molt, the birds may improve in color, cock birds especially.

There are three mutations in the Star Finch, namely the Yellow, the Pied, and the Fawn. I have not seen examples of the latter. The Yellow is well established and a reasonable number are being bred each year. Coloration is as for the Normal, except that the areas which would be red in the Normal are yellow-orange in the Yellow mutation.

Pied Stars have been available in the UK since about 1985, all originating from Europe. It is an attractive mutation, but at present the pied areas only seem to appear on the extremities, i.e., the head, wings, and tail. For the mutation to become universally popular, the pied areas need to appear on the actual body also. In adult birds the pied areas on the head and wings are lemon in the cocks and pale lemon in the hens; the tail feathers of both sexes, if pied, are pink. In the Pied Stars I have bred, the red on the head appears to mask out most of the pied feathering. This is unfortunate as it means that an immature cock bird, which may have practically the whole of the head pied, once adult, loses all the pied area which in a Normal bird would be red. Immature birds, if heavily pied around the head, may have white or partly white beaks, but here again, once the bird reaches maturity, the red of the beak (as with the feathers) masks out the pied area.

STRESS

Birds that are forced to live in a continual state of stress can quickly succumb to diseases which would not have taken hold had the cause of stress been eliminated the moment it became apparent. It is difficult to describe stress symptoms, as each individual may show them in a different manner. However, aviary birds which continually hide away or are seen to cling to the wires of the flight may be suffering from stress and a careful watch should be maintained to ensure that such birds are not being harassed by others with which they are housed.

A certain amount of bickering is almost certain to occur in an aviary containing more than one pair of birds. If the birds are all fit and healthy, then such squabbles should have little effect. However, a bird that is continually harassed should be removed, especially if the remainder of the inmates appear to be living together amicably. A bird that is seen to bully others continually should also be removed, as, due to stress, its more docile companions may eventually lose condition and then become susceptible to disease.

The above applies equally to birds housed in communal indoor flights.

Caged birds are not as susceptible to stress, especially when housed in pairs. It is important, however, to ensure that breeding pairs are compatible, as if one member of the pair becomes stressed through continual harassment from its companion, there will be little hope of the pair breeding successfully. I have always found it preferable to place a breeding pair in their quarters at the same time, although it is possible to place a cock bird in the breeding cage a few days before the hen is introduced. Indeed, such a procedure sometimes helps the cock to assert himself and then, when the hen is eventually introduced, the cock bird will, if in breeding condition, immediately begin to display. If a hen is placed in a breeding cage first and the cock is introduced a few days later, the hen will often reject him; indeed, she may dominate him in such a way that he is continually under stress, and, unless removed, he may eventually die.

Often bird keepers themselves subject their birds to stress when a little thought could avoid such situations. Entering the birds' quarters in unfamiliar clothing can cause stress, as can appearing without warning. Before entering my birdroom, I always give a light tap on the door. Should I forget to do so, it is obvious that my sudden appearance has caused stress to the birds as many will give alarm signals. Incubating birds may even leave the nest. Once the birds see who it is, they settle down almost immediately, nevertheless they have, for a few moments, been caused unnecessary stress.

Many breeders will not allow strangers into their birdrooms or near their aviaries if their birds are breeding. I have rarely gone as far as this, but do insist that visitors move around quietly and do not lean up against cages or aviaries. Also, I insist that items that may prove frightening to the birds are not held in the hands or left anywhere in the birdroom. Even such an everyday item as a lady's handbag can cause stress; indeed, I remember such an item so terrifying a pet parrot I once owned that it fell from its perch with shock!

Catching birds can also cause stress. It is inevitable that birds have to be caught from time to time, but this should be accomplished as quickly and as quietly as possible. If a net is used, it should not be waved around indiscriminately, but should be held close to the body until one is actually ready to catch the bird required. Aviary birds can prove extremely difficult to catch and, if at all possible, traps should be used rather than nets, especially if any of the birds are breeding (see CATCHING).

SYDNEY WAXBILL (see RED-BROWED FINCH)

T

TEMPERATURE

In my opinion no species of Australian finch can be kept and persuaded to breed successfully unless supplied with heated quarters during the colder months of the year. In tropical or subtropical regions, where there is little variation in temperature throughout the year, Australian finches can, of course, be housed permanently in unheated accommodation. However, even in certain parts of Australia heat would be required during the colder months.

The Gouldian Finch is a species that revels in heat, and from my experience this species can be exposed to temperatures so high that few other species could endure them. For the Gouldian, a temperature of 18°C (64°F) is recommended. Such species as Stars, Bichenos, Plum-headed, and Crimson Finches can also be kept at a temperature of approximately 18°C; this can be lowered to around 15°C (59°F) out of the breeding season. The more robust species, such as Long-tails, Heck's, Chestnut-breasteds, Blue-faced Parrot Finches, Black-throated (Parsons), etc., can be kept at lower temperatures, but I would suggest the minimum should be 15°C.

As mentioned under HEATING, the ideal way in which to heat a birdroom is by using an electric fan heater which is connected to a reliable thermostat. When the outside temperature is sufficient to allow the heating to be disconnected, one should take the opportunity to clean and service the heater and thermostat thoroughly. Both could then be stored in a polyethylene bag ready for immediate use as required (see ELECTRICAL INSTALLATION).

TRANSPORTATION

Newly purchased birds, or those which are being transported for some other reason, should be carried in such a way as to cause as little stress as possible. If birds are

A two-tier transporting cage.

to be sent by rail or road transport, then the correct procedures must be carried out. Nowadays certain rules must be adhered to if birds are to be transported: the recommended boxes must be used (otherwise the carrier will almost certainly refuse to take the birds); also, the birds can only be en route for a certain number of hours. The onus is on the person dispatching the birds, not the carrier, therefore it is up to you, the bird keeper, to ensure that you are aware of the rules that apply before attempting to have birds dispatched.

When purchasing new stock, it is, if at all possible, preferable to collect the birds yourself rather than have them dispatched by carrier or by rail. A show cage or something similar should be taken along, as to place newly purchased birds in any old box that comes to hand is certainly not the ideal way to transport them, especially if a long journey is to be undertaken. Food should be supplied, the ideal being a piece of spray millet taped to the rear wall of the cage, next to a perch. Even for a long journey,

there is little need to supply water for drinking. However, water should be offered the moment you arrive home with the birds.

Birds must not be placed in the trunk of a car under any circumstances, but should be placed in the rear of the car on the seat. If the car is a hatch-back, then the birds could be placed in the luggage area as long as the rear window shelf has been removed. If there are no passengers in the car, then the birds could be placed on the front seat. Wherever they are placed, the cage(s) must be made secure, otherwise, should the driver have to brake suddenly, the cages could topple off a seat, causing much stress to the birds. Upon arriving home with the birds (be they from a carrier or collected direct from a breeder or supplier), if it is late in the evening it would be best if the birds were offered food and water and left in the container or cage in which they have been transported. The following morning they could be released into a holding cage for observation. If you feel that, no matter how late in the evening it is, the birds would be more settled if released into a holding cage, then the birdroom lights would need to be left on for a while; at least until the newly acquired stock had been given a chance first to feed and then to settle on a perch for sleep (see PURCHASING STOCK).

TWIRLING
This is a nervous disorder to which Australian finches are sometimes prone. The Gouldian Finch, in particular, can suffer from this disorder. An affected bird will be seen to throw back its head and rotate it; in severe cases, the affected bird may fall from the perch, rotating the whole of its body while crouching on the floor. Severe attacks may cause death.

A suggested cure is to administer Vitamin B directly into the affected bird's beak. Birds showing signs of this disorder should never be used for breeding as they may pass on the complaint to their offspring.

WATER (BATHING) (see BATHING)

WATER (DRINKING)
Birds that are permanently supplied with bathing facilities may rarely drink the water supplied specifically for drinking. Nevertheless, it should always be available. The easiest way in which to offer drinking water to caged birds and those housed in indoor flights is to use clip-on founts, which can be attached to the cage front or the wire of the flight, in both cases near to a perch. Clip-on founts are available from the majority of dealers in aviary products. Obviously the same type of drinker can be utilized for aviary birds, however most bird keepers may prefer to supply drinking water in jam jar founts or something similar, as not only would these be easier to site in an aviary, but they also take a larger volume of water.

Should you decide to supply vitamins to your stock, there are numerous water-soluble additives on the market and the correct dosage is usually printed on the container label. As already mentioned, birds that have bathing water permanently available may rarely take water from the drinkers. If this is the case, and you particularly want your birds to drink the water to which vitamins have been added, the bathing receptacles would have to be removed from time to time, thus forcing the birds to take water from the drinkers.

WHITE-EARED GRASSFINCH
(*Poephila personata leucotis*)
The White-eared Grassfinch is a subspecies of the Masked, and whereas the latter has ear coverts, breast, and flanks of a sandy-buff color, the White-eared has, as the name suggests, white ear coverts with midflanks and the breast pinkish-buff. The approximate length is 130–140 mm (5–5½ in). It is found in Cape York Peninsula, west to the Leichardt river.

A selection of water drinkers. Note that the spherical container (right) can also be adapted for use as a seedhopper (left). However, it should be noted that not all keepers favor the use of seed hoppers.

The White-eared is extremely rare in aviculture, even in its country of origin. It is not available in the USA or UK.

YELLOW-RUMPED FINCH
(*Lonchura flaviprymna*) (color photos on page 94)

The approximate overall length is 110 mm (4¼ in). Adults are gray on the head and more whitish on the sides of the face and the bib. The mantle is chestnut; the rump and upper-tail coverts are yellow. The tail is yellowish; the breast and abdomen are white, tinged with yellow on the flanks. The under-tail coverts are black. The beak is bluish-gray.

This mannikin has a restricted distribution from the eastern Kimberley region in Western Australia to western Arnhem Land in the Northern Territory. It is found mainly in the Ord, Daly, and upper Roper river systems. It frequents tall grasses on the margins of swamps, reedbeds, and mangroves.

As well as being relatively rare in the wild, the Yellow-rumped Finch is far from abundant in aviculture (even in Australia). It is a large robust mannikin which deserves to be more widely kept than it is. Sexing is, without doubt, extremely difficult (the cock is said to have a more silvery-gray sheen to the head than the hen), however, as with the Chestnut-breasted Finch (to which it is closely related), the Yellow-rumped could, no doubt, be sexed more readily by the song of the cock bird. (See SEXING and also MONOMORPHIC SPECIES.)

Aviary accommodation is probably the most suitable for this species, nevertheless it will breed in a roomy box cage. If housed in an aviary with other species, no other mannikins should be included, otherwise hybrids may be produced.

The normal clutch averages four or five eggs. Both birds take turns in incubating, but only the hen sits during the night. The eggs hatch some 12 to 14 days after incubation begins and the chicks leave the nest when they are approximately three weeks old. They become independent at around five to six weeks after hatching. Immature birds are dark brown on the upperparts and buffish-gray on the underparts, with a dull yellow rump. Adult plumage is not attained until the birds are some five months of age.

Breeding pairs will rear young on a diet of seeds alone, however it is beneficial to offer live food in the form of mealworms or live ants' eggs. Some pairs may also be persuaded to sample soft food.

There are no known mutations in the Yellow-rumped Finch, which is not surprising when one considers the small numbers bred each year.

Z

ZEBRA FINCH (*Poephila guttata*)
Although this species is widely distributed throughout Australia, the Zebra Finch (sometimes given the scientific name *Taeniopygia guttata*) is fully domesticated and has a niche in aviculture all of its own. Because of this, it is rarely included in a book devoted to the avicultural aspect of Australian finches.

Being as keen to nest and raise young as the Society Finch, the Zebra is sometimes used as a foster for deserted eggs or chicks from other Australian finches. Zebra Finches will successfully rear chicks of other species, but as they are not as reliable as Society Finches, it is not a practice I recommend. Under no circumstances, however, should Zebra Finches be used as fosters for Bicheno Finch chicks, as, being closely related and so much alike in their habits, there is every possibility that the Bicheno chicks would become imprinted on their Zebra Finch fosters and, because of this, refuse to mate later on with their own kind (see IMPRINTING).

The Zebra is a firm favorite with many fanciers throughout the world and specialist societies exist in the majority of countries where aviculture is practiced. Over the years, a number of excellent books devoted entirely to the Zebra Finch have been published, and many are still in print. Because the Zebra Finch is widely covered in such literature, and as the majority of enthusiasts would require far more detailed information than it would be possible to give here, I shall refrain from discussing the species further, except to mention that of all the Australian finches, the Zebra has the most mutations, with new ones appearing almost annually.

Normal Zebra Finch (cock).

144